DE CONTROVERSIIS
CHRISTIANAE FIDEI
ADVERSUS HUIUS TEMPORIS
HAERETICOS

ON THE CONTROVERSIES OF
THE CHRISTIAN FAITH
AGAINST THE HERETICS
OF THIS TIME

ST. ROBERT BELLARMINE
OF THE SOCIETY OF JESUS
DOCTOR OF THE CHURCH

TRANSLATED FROM
THE ORIGINAL LATIN BY

RYAN GRANT

MEDIATRIX PRESS

Generosus Roberti
Bellarmini
S.R.E.
Presbÿter
Cardinalis
Archiepisc.
Capua

Leody·I·Valdor sculp[e]b·

On the Marks of the Church
St. Robert Bellarmine, S.J.
Doctor of the Church

Translated from the Latin
of the 1588 Ingolstadt edition
by
Ryan Grant

MEDIATRIX PRESS

MMXV

ISBN-13: 978-0692368602

Translated from *De Notis Ecclesiae*
De Controversiis Christianae Fidei: Adversus Hujus Temporis Haereticos,
Tribus Tomis Comprehensae
Tomus II, Liber IV, De Ecclesia
Sertorius Publishers, Ingolstadt, 1588

Table of Contents

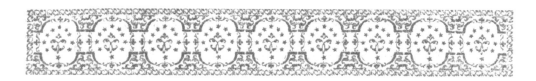

Translator's Preface

This is the first of any of St. Robert Bellarmine's dogmatic works to be translated into English. Some of his spiritual writings or sermons have been translated, such as his eschatological works on death, heaven and hell, and are published by TAN books, but the book you are holding in your hand is very special, the only one of its kind. It is also the first of many forthcoming translations of the corpus of Bellarmine's works.

St. Robert Bellarmine was one of the most important writers of the so-called "Counter-Reformation," as he took up the task of answering the major Protestant writers directly and fully on numerous subjects. He was not the first, but indeed was the most systematic, drawing on the works of many great writers before him, such as St. John Fisher, St. Peter Canisius, Thomas Stapleton, and the German writer John Cochlaeus. Before Canisius or Bellarmine, St. John Fisher was perhaps the best and most able writer against Luther, something that is almost forgotten today as his works refuting Luther's doctrine remain in Latin and long out of print, though they may be acquired in scanned copies from 16th and 17th century prints. The problem in the later half of the 16th century was that, even though no Protestant had ever attempted a refutation of St. John Fisher, the issues at hand had multiplied. In the first place, Fisher had ably refuted Luther, and other Lutheran authors such as Zwingli and Oecolampadius, but had not yet written a refutation of Calvin when he was cut down by Henry VIII. Moreover, numerous other writers had appeared, names that are forgotten by us today, but were prolific in their own time, such as John of Brenz, Peter Martyr, Theodore Beza, and the Lutheran Centuriators of Magdeburg. The bar had moved sharply, and following the Council of Trent, Protestant writers focused their energies on new subjects, though following the fundamental principles of Luther's twin heresies: *sola fide* and *sola scriptura*.

St. Robert Bellarmine then, in taking up the challenge of his day, drew from the works of numerous other writers and was willing to do what most were not, quote the Protestants at length, and then refute them at length, which is the same method that St. John Fisher had followed so profitably a generation before. Bellarmine began, however, not with the aim of writing formal treatises against the Protestants, but rather teaching young seminarians how to refute them. Towards the end of the 16th century, he became the first lecturer of

Controversial Theology at the Roman College, a task that had been attempted twice previously, but without success. Bellarmine surpassed everyone's hopes, and outdid himself with his vast knowledge of the Fathers of the Church, combined with his mastery of the Protestant authors themselves. It was suggested to him in 1586 that he should transform his notes into books for the benefit of all. This was duly completed, and the first volume appeared in 1588. The reception was overwhelmingly positive, and the works proved a great fruit not only to preachers, but even to effect the conversion of Protestants who read them. Not everyone was pleased, however. The method of quoting the Protestants so often did not please everyone. One fellow Jesuit remarked that one need not bother reading the Protestant authors, you can find all their works in Bellarmine. Yet the work was so complete and challenging, that the Calvinist theologian, Junius, reckoned: "Methinks it is not one Bellarmine who speaks in these pages. It is the whole Jesuit phalanx, the entire legion of them mustered for our destruction."[1] Of course it was not so. The humble Italian Jesuit of relatively short height would dominate the apologetic scene as long as the Latin tongue held sway.

Thus we have begun with this work, On the Marks of the Church, as a starting point, though it by no means is *the* starting point of his works.

This is for editorial reasons. It is a shorter work than most in the controversies, and it is a good introduction to Bellarmine's style on an important subject. Bellarmine does not write on the Marks as given in the Creed: One, Holy, Catholic and Apostolic; rather he continues the work of the theologians of that day in unpacking those four, and developing their consequences in other areas. Thus, in this work, Bellarmine gives 15 Marks of the True Church which can be visibly discerned in history, and uses these to refute Protestant teaching, though they can all be referred back to the aforesaid Four Marks.

Now, a word must be said on the term "Mark." The Latin word is *Nota*, and thus, used to be translated as "Note" by the theologians. *Nota* is from the verb *novisse*, and means "a thing known," or "a thing that something is known by." Yet, since the mid-twentieth century, it has been standard to say the "marks of the Church." So there was a quandary... Do I translate this literally, and in my view, properly, as "note," or more familiarly as "mark?" In fine, "mark" was chosen for the sake of ease for modern readers. Thus my apologies to those who would rather see it as "note."

A word must also be said about footnotes. In Bellarmine's day, this textual

---

[1] Brodrick, *Robert Bellarmine, Saint and Scholar*, pg. 76, Neuman Press, 1961.

device had not yet been developed. Notes were often put in margins or within the text. In *The Controversies*, Bellarmine provides his notes, be they of Scripture or of an author, within the text. For the modern reader, this seriously interrupts the flow of the reading, so I have placed these as footnotes within the text. At that, critical editions of the Fathers did not exist, and many of the works he refers to are only in Latin, or in the original languages of the authors, French, Dutch or German. Thus in footnoting, while conforming to modern style, I have used only the Latin title of the work in question without attempting the voluminous task of conforming the references to the Fathers to extant copies in English, should they exist at all. Much of the time the English retains its original Latin title, and it is not difficult to search for these on the internet. Other works, such as those of Luther, or the *Institutes* of Calvin, were written in both Latin and the vernacular, and may even be found in digitized form on the internet.

Lastly, I have followed the standard English custom of not capitalizing the pronouns for which God is the antecedent, as this is not normally done in scholarly works as it is in devotional books.

As in all my translations, I have endeavored to stay as true to the Latin as possible, even to the point of being slavish in some places, to avoid losing the meaning of a given point, though not so slavish as to retain the endless participle phrases and the "therefore" of every sentence which is such a hallmark of good Latin rhetorical style. Any glosses for clarification are relegated to footnotes, which are simply marked as "-Translator's note."

Lastly, but most importantly, this work, as well as future works, would not be possible without those who have generously donated money to accomplish this project. It has been supported via a page on the website Go Fund Me, which can be found here: http://www.gofundme.com/RobertBellarmine. Without the kind assistance of these benefactors, no matter how small, I could not have labored on this, and would have no hope of being able to complete any future works. If you wish to monetarily support future translations of St. Robert Bellarmine's dogmatic works, then please visit the above mentioned website.

As the four hundredth anniversary of the Reformation approaches, there is much confusion in the Church, even to the point where some suggest we can learn from the "Reformers," or even worse, that it is said in some Catholic circles that "Luther got it right." Bellarmine would disagree, for the clear reasons elucidated in texts such as these. Such sentiments arise from largely the same fault as was committed by the leaders of the Reformation themselves, the inability to distinguish between the man and the office. Just as the Church was in need of reform prior to that event, so much more is it in need of reform today. The difference, however, is that the erudition is sorely lacking today compared with Bellarmine's time. People no longer read Latin, and as such the works of the great theologians which were once disseminated, read, commented on and preached from the Latin are now lost. It is my supreme hope that this project will contribute to the continuing reform of the Church, by providing those who cannot read Latin, let alone have the access to the works of the great theologians such as St. Robert Bellarmine, to grasp that clear explication of the Church's perennial teaching, passed on by Christ to the apostles, and by the apostles to the Church with the ever present assistance of the Spirit of truth, promised to remain with the Church even to the consummation of the age. The importance of the great theologians like Bellarmine and others whom we could name endlessly, is that they worked from principles, and followed from those principles with the clear teaching of what the Church has always and everywhere believed, solidly based in the Fathers of the Church and the historic witness of faith passed on by the Church. This is no mere project of antiquarian interest, but part of the patrimony of Catholic thought which should be available to all, for the deepening of their faith and the striving to what the Church is but a figure, that dwelling in the presence of God face to face to which it is ordered.

Ryan Grant
Post Falls, ID
Winter 2014

CHAPTER I
A Treatise on the Marks of the Church is of Great Profit

E turn to the Controversy on the Marks of the true Church, which is a very useful controversy. For, everyone affirms that the true faith, the true remission of sins, the true hope of eternal salvation, can be found in the true Church alone. It is so clear that St. Cyprian said: "They cannot remain with God, who refuse to remain as one in the Church of God. Although they may burn with a flame, indeed they have been handed over to the fire, or being cast out they place their souls before wild beasts; for them there will be no crown of faith, rather the punishment of the faithless: such can be killed, but not crowned."[2]

All the Fathers teach alike, and even the heretics do not deny this. Therefore on that account, every heresy treats itself alone as the true Church, and all others it places outside the Church, as Lactantius teaches in these words: "It is only the Catholic Church which retains true worship. Further, this is the font of truth, this is the household of faith, the temple of God, whereby, if anyone will not have entered, or if one would have gone out from it, he is a stranger to the hope of life and eternal salvation. Nevertheless, five individual sects of heretics reckon that they are the true Christians, and that their Church is Catholic."[3] Therefore, if we should agree on this controversy, all the rest might be settled easily. Two things must be dealt with. In the first place, the opinion of today's heretics on the marks of the Church must be refuted. Secondly, the Catholic teaching on them must be explained and defended.

---

[2] Cyprian, *De simplicitate praelatorum.*

[3] Lactantius, Lib 4, cap. Ult. divinarum institutionum.

Chapter II

The Teachings of the Heretics are refuted.

THUS unto the first. Luther, in the book *On Councils and the Church*, in the last part of the book proposes these seven marks. Firstly, the true and incorrupt preaching of the Gospel. Second, the administration of baptism. Third, the legitimate use of the Eucharist. Fourth, the legitimate use of the keys. Fifth, the legitimate election of ministers, in order that they should teach and administer the sacraments. Sixth, public preaching, and psalmody, as well as catechism, but in a language which can be understood by all. Seventh, and lastly, the mystery of the cross, that is, the tribulations within and without, so that inwardly there might be sorrow, pusillanimity, and terror; outside poverty, contempt and that they might be held by all men as heretics, servants of demons, and Cathars.

It must be noted that Luther is exceedingly careful lest he might take any of those marks which are in the creed of Constantinople; since all the ancient councils wished to distinguish themselves from all other sects by those marks, especially through "Apostolic Church." Next, the remainder usually propose only two, which embrace the first five marks of Luther, that is, the sincere preaching of the word of God, and sincere use of the sacraments; and from these two each sect "proves" itself to be the true Church. The Augsburg confession teaches thus, in article 6 and in the defense of the same. Likewise, John of Brenz in the Wittenberg Confession, on the chapter on the Church, as well as John Calvin in the Institutes,[4] and the Centurators of Magdeburg[5] add two others to these two, which can be reduced to the fifth and seventh of Luther. That is, constancy in the confession of faith (or perseverance), and obedience toward the ministers of the word, in so far as they administer the word.

---

[4] *Instit.*, Bk 4, ch. 1 §9, 10 and 11.

[5] *Cent. 1*, lib. 1, ch. 4, col. 137 and 174; *Cent. 1* lib. 2, ch. 4, column 379, 380 and 381. [The Centuriators of Magdeburg were a group of Lutherans who attempted to show through historical tracts that Lutheranism was the religion of the early Church, and it was supplanted by the Catholic Church after the first five centuries, and was so until Luther's time when it was restored. They were amply refuted by St. Peter Canisius, S.J., and Cardinal Baronius, and even amongst Protestants today they are but little more than antiquarian interest. -Translator's note].

These notes are not in any way sufficient. In the first place, they do not declare what the true Church might be according to the heretics, rather what it probably might be; consequently we cannot know who the elect might be, or the just, and chiefly we learn where the Church might hide, rather than where it might be. Besides, nor does this sufficiently reveal it. It can easily be proved from individuals.

To the first, it is so for three reasons. First of all, the marks ought to be proper and not common. If I should wish to describe a certain man for you, whom you have never seen, so that when you will see him you may pick him out from a crowd, I ought *not* to say that there is a fellow who has two eyes, two hands, etc., for these are common to all. Nor even ought I to designate him through marks which, although they might be proper according to an individual, they are not proper in the opinion of others, since many usually claim these for themselves. Thus, he who is sought would never be discovered.

To be sure, sincere preaching of truth is a mark common to all sects, at least in their own opinion. For, either preaching ought to be pure from all error, or only made from essentials and fundamentals.

If the first should be given, we can gather from this very mark that the Church is among none of the Lutherans; for it is they themselves who affirm their Churches are not without blemish. Luther, in his book on the Church, clearly says that the word of God is a mark, although it is preached more in some places and in others less, and Calvin affirms the same thing.[6] If the second, already it will be a mark common to many sects.

Certainly the Lutherans and Zwinglians do not disagree on a particular fundamental of faith, as on the Trinity or the Incarnation. Nay more, even the Pelagians thought they had a "true Church," who in their primary articles did not disagree, before they gave birth to Nestorians. Even Coelestinus (as we learn from St. Augustine)[7] tried to show that he was not outside the Church, and yet, the Lutherans and Calvinists detest nothing more than the Pelagians; rather, they set us outside the Church before all, because they reckon us Pelagians.

In addition to this second mode, in the very matter there are some who do not agree with this mark, like the Anabaptists; nevertheless it is asserted by all in one opinion. What sect was there ever which did not say that it held the true preaching of truth? Certainly St. Augustine says that the Catholic Church is recognized easily by many marks, but the heretics have nothing except the

---

[6] *Inst.*, Bk 4 ch. 1 § 12.

[7] *De peccato originali*, Bk 2 ch. 22.

4

promise of truth, that is, what might be among them the truth, and sincere preaching.[8]

Secondly, the marks ought to be more familiar in that matter whose marks they are, otherwise they are not known at all, rather unknown. Now, our adversaries do not only want external preaching to be a mark of the Church, but preaching and reception. There indeed the true Church is, they say, where the word is preached, heard and believed. But who can know where the word is truly believed? Wherefore, the same holds concerning external preaching. Without a doubt what the true Church may be is more knowable than what the true preaching of the word might be; for we learn this from the Church, as Irenaeus, Tertullian, Augustine and all the Fathers teach.

Irenaeus said: "Why, truly even if on some modest question dispute were to arise, wouldn't it be fitting to hasten to the oldest Churches, and to take up the question at hand from them, which is in the matter certain and pure?"[9] Tertullian likewise: "The apostles preached what Christ had revealed to them, and here I put forth that nothing ought to be proved otherwise, than through these same Churches, which the apostles themselves built: if these are so, it is certain hence that every doctrine found with those apostolic Churches agrees with the root and origins of faith, it must be reckoned true, the rest that does not ought to be written off as lies."[10] It is shown by the same reason; for true preaching is preaching, and interpretation of the true divine scriptures; what might be the true scriptures, however, and what might be their true sense, we cannot know, except from the testimony of the true Church, as Augustine teaches.[11] Even John of Brenz himself, in the Wittenberg confession, affirms that the Church has the right of testimony on true scripture, and even of interpreting the true scripture. Furthermore, Calvin wishes the Church to be the faithful watchman of the word of God,[12] and Philip Melanchthon in *Locis capite de Ecclesia* requires the testimony of the true Church to impose a decision on lawsuits. But first, the guardian of the treasure ought to be known, rather than

---

[8] Augustine, *Contra epistolam fundamenti*, ch. 4.

[9] Irenaeus, bk. 3, ch. 4.

[10] Tertullian, *De praescript contra hereticos*.

[11] Augustine, *Contra epist. Fundamenti*, ch. 5; *de utilitate credendi*, ch. 14.

[12] Bk. 4, ch. 1 § 5.

the treasure; and the teacher more than the doctrine, although doctrine is sought from a teacher, not the other way around. Therefore, the Church is a mark of true preaching, rather than true preaching a mark of the Church.

Third, the true marks are inseparable from the true Church, but the Churches of the Corinthians and Galatians, to whom Paul wrote, were true Churches, and nevertheless there was not in those Churches true preaching at a certain time, as can be understood from the apostle, who says he is writing to the Churches of God, which are at Corinth, or in Galatia, where he complains that at Corinth, because some taught there would not be a resurrection, and at Galatia nearly the whole epistle scolds them, because they taught that they must keep the law of Moses with the gospel.

But you say, how were these true Churches, when they taught heresy? I respond: It is one thing to err, and be prepared to learn, and when you will learn, to obey; it is another to wish not to learn, and when you will have learned the truth, to refuse to acquiesce. Neither of these can be in the universal Church; in a particular Church, however, there can be the first, in neither the universal Church nor a particular Church the second, rather only in the synagogue of Satan, and in Churches of the wicked. Again, there can be a doctrine pure from all other error in a false Church; for schismatics, such as the Luciferians and Donatists, from the beginning held the whole doctrine, and nevertheless were outside the Church. If they should say they do not have the whole doctrine, because true doctrine teaches one must remain in the unity of the true Church, or the converse, since schismatics believe and teach that it behooves one to be in the true Church and to obey the true head, although they do not do it; and hence they do not err in faith, rather they fail in charity. Yet, schism, if it should endure for long, will at length sink into heresy.

Still, John of Brenz, Philip Melanchthon and Calvin object on behalf of this mark, making use of certain places of Scripture: "My sheep will hear my voice."[13] Therefore, there is a Church, where the word of God is heard. Likewise, they appeal to Ephesians V: "Cleansing her by the washing in the word of life."[14] The Church is cleansed in the word, therefore wherever the cleansing word is, there is the Church. So Melanchthon argues in his *apologia*. Calvin, however, concentrates on Matthew XVIII: "Where there are two or three, etc."[15]

---

[13] John X: 27.

[14] Ephes. V: 26.

[15] *Instit.*, bk. 4, ch. 1 § 9.

Brenz produces that from John X:35: "He called them gods, to whom the word of God was spoken." And in the next chapter, "You are clean, on account of the word, which I spoke to you." [John XV:3]. That, indeed, is the Church, which is clean in the presence of God. And that of Romans: "The gospel is the power of God for the salvation of all believers." [Romans I:16]. Chrysostom adds: "Whoever therefore wishes to recognize which Church may be the true Church of Christ, from where shall he do so, unless only through the Scriptures?"[16] And Augustine: "We learn of Christ in the Scriptures, we learn of the Church in the scriptures," etc. In like manner, we also find from Augustine: "The question turns about among us, where the Church might be; what, therefore, are we going to do in our words intending to seek that, or in the words of its chapters? I reckon what chiefly in those words we ought to seek, which is truth, and knows its body best." Lastly, from the same: "Let us not hear: I say these things, you say these things, but let us hear: thus says the Lord . . . I refuse the documents of men, rather that the holy Church be proved from the divine precepts."[17]

I respond. The first citation does not teach where the Church might be, but teaches who might be the elect, without a doubt those who steadfastly hear from the heart, and retain the word, as St. Augustine shows; although, since it cannot be known who it is in fact that hears with their heart, this cannot be a visible mark of the Church, but is a mark of each individually, that conjecturally one might recognize his election.

The second citation proves nothing; for that cleansing is invisible, nor does Paul wish to teach in that place, what may be or where may be the Church, but what good God will have conferred to the Church.

The third citation does not show where the Church might be, but where Christ may be. Where, indeed, is the true Church, there is Christ. Besides, if it were a mark of the Church to be gathered in the name of Christ, then certainly it will not be to be gathered in just any way in the name of Christ, for even all heretics and schismatics are gathered in the name of Christ. Rather, it will be gathered by those who exercise the authority of Christ, such as are legitimately ordained bishops, and those succeeding them, and so on and so forth back to the apostles, whom Christ at first left behind in His place. Thus in that way such a mark would coincide with ours, which we will take up later on.

The fourth citation proves nothing. Firstly, because there, only princes are

---

[16] *In Matth.*, Hom. 49.

[17] *Epist. 166; De Utilitate Credendi; de unitate Ecclesiae*, ch. 2; *ibid* ch. 3.

called gods, to whom God consigned something; therefore, that word of God is to be made to some purpose. Secondly, because the word of God does not make gods, if it is merely preached, but if it should be received and believed: but this is invisible, as is obvious.

The fifth place is like unto the second, wherein the same Brenz says the Church is clean in the sight of God, that is not in the sight of men; and he does not notice from this mark follows, that it becomes manifest to God, not to us.

The sixth place proves nothing; for the effect of the Gospel is invisible.

Yet Calvin presses on. The word of God is fruitful, and wherever it is preached, it increases, therefore wherever it is preached, there is some Church.

I respond. If this reasoning proves something, it merely proves that where it is preached, there are some good men; but we do not know them. Morever, it doesn't prove this; for the word of God always increases when legitimately preached; it is by the ordinary power from those preachers who were sent. Besides, we see it preached among heretics in various sects where it does not increase unless by mistake. As to the citation from St. John Chrysostom, we have already responded to it often. Rather I will concentrate on the citations from St. Augustine. It is proven from Scripture where the Church may be, not from a mark of the Church as it were, but because Scripture teaches what might be known as long as it teaches, what kind it might be, where it began, and how it increased.

You will say, "at least Scripture is more known than the Church, seeing that therein the Church is proved."

I respond. Considered simply, the Church is earlier and more known than the Scripture is. For the Church was before Scripture, and the Scripture was given to it by God, She hands it down to others, and explains it: nevertheless, at some time hypothetically the Scripture was better known when obviously Scripture was received, and speaks clearly and a question arises on the Church itself. As now and then on the other side the Church was received, and known, and a question arises on Scripture: and thus one is proved from the other. When the grace of the word was disputed on the baptism of heretics, because Scripture speaks obscurely, and the Church was known, Augustine proved, according to the Scriptures, that the baptism of heretics was valid, because the Church held it as valid. On the other hand, when it was disputed on the Church, whether the Church was in Africa alone, because the Scriptures were received and clear, Augustine proved from them; and we do the same thing when we deduce the marks of the Church from the Scripture, but it is not for the reason that they are simply more known than the Church.

The second mark is refuted by the same arguments. For all claim the same for themselves: apart from Catholics, Calvinists are separated from the Lutherans, because they both think that they alone have the true sacrament of the Eucharist. The Anabaptists, however, are separated from both, because they think they alone have the true use of baptism. On that account the Pelagians held all the sacraments, and likewise all the schismatics. Secondly, the legitimate use of the sacraments is less known than the Church might be. For this is the legitimate use of the sacraments, which is in conformity with Scripture, as they teach themselves. Yet the Scriptures depend on the Church, not the other way around, as we have often said. Thirdly, the Church at Corinth was a true Church, and nevertheless they are scolded, because they did not treat certain sacraments purely,[18] as were likewise the African Churches, which were under Cyprian, and under those eighty six bishops, whose teachings he says were of the true Church, as St. Augustine and St. Jerome also teach.[19] They did not purely treat the sacrament of baptism as the same Jerome and Augustine teach.

The third mark must be refuted, that is prayer and psalmody, which is the sixth Lutheran mark. It is refuted, because if one should speak on invocation, which proceeds from the heart, it is an invisible mark. Moreover, if one speaks on an external invocation and psalmody, it is a very common mark. For all sects at this time, even the Anabaptists, say the Lord's prayer, and sing the psalms in the vernacular, even the Arians long ago did the same thing, as Socrates relates,[20] as well as Ambrose.[21] Nay more, it can almost be said, that at this time to sing the psalms in Latin is a mark of the true Church, because this seems to be a relic of antiquity alone, and of the universal Church, which is not changed daily as the sects of heretics.

The fourth mark is refuted, which is the seventh Lutheran mark, without a doubt; internal sorrow, pusillanimity, external persecutions and to be called heretics. With respect to being internal, as a mark it is very false, since if they are internal, they are obscure. Likewise, pusillanimity is a vice, and Paul everywhere exhorts to internal joy, and says the kingdom of God is joyful in the

---

[18] 1 Corinthians XI.

[19] Augustine, *De Baptismo*, bk. 6, ch. 7; Jerome, *Contra Luciferianos.*

[20] Lib. 6, c. 8.

[21] *De Tradendis basilicis.*

Holy Spirit.[22] With respect to externals, it is not a perpetual mark, for the Church in the beginning and in the end suffered great difficulties: but in the midst it was in bloom, and everything was predicted.[23]

The fifth mark is of the Centuriators of Magdeburg, that it would be the true Church in which they are found who persevere in the confession of faith even to death. Such is refuted firstly, because confession of the true faith is no more a mark than the true preaching of the Scriptures, and the legitimate use of the sacraments.

Secondly, because a true Church could not be gathered in any way by the Lutherans. These say that for many centuries before the coming of Luther, the confession of true faith ceased, and the Church was preserved in hiding, and was altogether invisible, therefore the Church of the Lutherans is new, and hence false.

Thirdly, because we see this mark in all sects, and no less than in the body of Lutherans; for in the first years our Church has innumerable martyrs, who persevered steadfastly in the confession of faith; thereupon the Montanists exceedingly boasted of their martyrs, as can be seen both from Eusebius[24] and Tertulian[25], the latter who wrote while he was a Montanist against Catholics, objecting against them that they had acted wickedly by fleeing persecution.

Likewise, Massalians with Epiphanius,[26] who says they also had martyrs, for they boasted much in their number. The same is certain of the Donatists, as St. Augustine says: "Those who lived as thieves, they honored as martyrs."[27] On the Anabaptists who lived at the time of St. Bernard, he writes: "Some marvel that not only patiently, but even happily they were lead to death."[28] Aeneas Sylvius

---

[22] See Romans XIV, Coloss. III, Philipp. IV, Ephes. V.

[23] See St. Augustine, *Epist. 50.*

[24] *Hist.* Bk 5, ch. 18.

[25] *De fuga in persequutione.*

[26] *Haeres.* 80.

[27] *Epist.* 68.

[28] *in Cantica,* Serm. 66.

[later Pope Pius II] wrote about the Adamites, "men joined with women, happy and usually singing to be rushed to the fire.[29] "In our time, no one is ignorant that in this obstinacy of dying for faithlessness, the Anabaptists hold first place, second the Calvinists, and well-nigh no pure Lutherans, who, nevertheless, propose this as a mark of the true Church.

---

[29] *De hist. Boemorum*, ch. 41.

Chapter III
The True Marks of the Church are Proposed

SINCE we have briefly refuted these "marks," it remains that we should propose the true marks. It must be observed from the beginning, however, that the Catholic Church is as a sun, which diffuses its most beautiful rays of light from every side, that it can be recognized very easily through them. Indeed, it has many marks, or testimonies, and signs, which discern her from every false religion of the Pagans, of Jews, and Heretics. Indeed, they do not evidently cause truth: she is the true Church of God, but nevertheless they cause it to be evidently believable, for it is not the same thing to be evidently true and evidently believable. For something to be called evidently true, it must appear to be either in itself, or in its principles. For something to be called evidently believable, it does not need to appear so in itself, or in its principles, nevertheless it has so many and such serious testimonies, that any wise man you like rightly ought to believe it. It is as though a judge should see a man to be killed by a thief, or lethally wounded and dies afterward, he has the evidence of truth, that the thief is a murderer; if however, he might not have seen the killing done, but might have twenty serious men as witnesses, who say they saw it, he has evidence of believability.

Therefore, we say the marks of the Church, which we produce, do not simply make the evidence of truth, because if that were so, no one could be found who would be able to deny it, just as you could find no one who would deny the teachings which the mathematicians prove; but, nevertheless, they cause the evidence of believability, according to the Psalm: "Your testimonies are exceedingly believable."[30] But among those who admit the Scriptures are divine, as well as the histories and the ancient writings of the Fathers, they even make evidence of truth. Even if the truth of articles of faith cannot be evident to us absolutely, nevertheless that truth can be evident hypothetically, that is, by supposing the truth of the Scriptures. The Scriptures being supposed, what is evidently deduced from the Scripture, is evidently true.

Next, these marks are called by various names, and St. Augustine places six

---

[30] Psalm XCII.

marks,[31] St. Jerome two,[32] St. Vincent of Lérin in his *Commonitorium*, three. From more recent writers, Driedo and Pedro de Soto[33] three others. Cardinal Hosius four.[34] Nicholas Sanders, six.[35] Miguel de Medina, eleven.[36] Gunter of Peter places twelve.[37]

We propose fifteen marks, which if anyone might wish, could be recalled to those four, which commonly and by more recent authors are assigned to the Constantinoplan creed, One, Holy, Catholic and Apostolic.

---

[31] *Contra epist. Fundamenti,* ch. 4.

[32] *Contra Luciferianos,* in fine.

[33] Driedo bk 4, ch. 2, part 2 *de Eccles. Dogmat.*; Pedro de Soto *Prima parte defensionis,* ch. 44 and following.

[34] *In explicatione symboli.*

[35] Bk 8 *de visibili monarchia,* ch. 50.

[36] Bk 2 *de recta fide.*

[37] *De notis Ecclesiae.*

THE FIRST MARK, is the very name of the Catholic and Christian Church; for, as St. Augustine teaches, even if every heresy should wish to appear and be called the Catholic Church, nevertheless, when the heretics are asked by the pagans where one would go to come together at a Catholic Church, none of them dares to show his house."[38] St. Cyril teaches, "If you will go out into some city, you do not ask where the Church might be, or the house of God, for even the heretics say theirs is the house of God, and the Church. Rather you ask, where might the Catholic Church be; that indeed is the proper name of this holy Church, the mother of us all; as if one might say, if you ask this, no heretic will show you his Church."[39]

Pacianus says, in his letter to Sympronianus, which is on the catholic name: "Certainly, that which has endured through so many centuries was not borrowed from men. That which you refer to as Catholic, does not denote Marcion, nor Apelles, nor Montanus, just as it does not suppose heretics as authors . . . My name is Christian, Catholic is my cognomen; that addresses me, that shows who I am." He says the same thing most beautifully, that the Catholic name agrees with the principle head and the trunk of that tree, from where many branches are cut off from different times: the heretical sects are the branches, that is, certain parts cut off from the tree of the Church: it is the very tree, which rests upon its root, as well as always remains the same, and Catholic is what the whole tree is called. Likewise, there is no heresy which would not take the name from some man as its author, and the Christian name should be abandoned by those who it leaves. Thus, in 1 Corinthians 3, some of the schismatics were saying: "I am of Paul, others, I am of Apollo, others, but I am of Cephas."

St. Justin Martyr says: "And they are distinct with respect to their cognomens, designated from certain men, since each one was the author of some new doctrine. Among them, some are called Marcionists, others Valentinians, others Basilidinians, other Saturinists, and others still by another

---

[38] Augustine, *Contra epist. Fundamenti*, ch. 4.

[39] *Cateches.* 18.

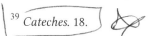

word, whatever it may be coming from the first inventor of their teaching."[40] Irenaeus adds: "They even have words, from Simon, the prince of the most impious teachings, which are called *Simony.*"[41] Lactantius says: "Although the Marcionists or the Arians are called Christians, those who have lost the name of Christ and clothed themselves in a human and external name, have ceased to be Christian."[42] St. Athanasius says against the Arians: "The people have never received a name from their bishops, but from the Lord, in whom they believed. Certainly we did not inherit names from the blessed apostles, but we are named after Christ because we are Christians. But they who deduce the origin of their faith from somewhere else rightly bear the names of their authors. For which reason, since we are all Christians and are called such, Marcion the inventor of his heresy is cast out. The rest who remain retain the title of Christians: those who followed Marcion were no longer Christians, but called Marcionists. Such is also the case with Valentinus, Basilides and Manes, and the others who bestowed names upon their sects."[43]

Chrysostom confirms this: "They have certain men after whom they are called: according to the name of the heresiarch, so also the sect is called, for us however, no man gave a name, rather the faith itself."[44]

Jerome says at the end of his work against the Luciferians: "If you will hear, in any place, those who are called Christians not by the Lord Jesus Christ but named after someone else, such as Marcionists or Valentinians; know that it is not the Church of Christ, but the synagogue of Antichrist." Today, therefore, if some are called "Martinists," or Lutherans, some Zwinglians, others Calvinists, etc., yet no one ever called us after some man, it is certain that ours is the true Church.

Wait a minute, they will say, everywhere you are called Papists, Romans, or Romanists. I respond: formerly Catholics were called "*homousians,*" but that word attested to truth. For these are not the names of some new author and heresiarch, as their names are: but *homousians* means one who believes the Son

---

[40] St. Justin Martyr, *Dialogue with Trypho.*

[41] Irenaeus, bk 1, ch. 20.

[42] Lactantius, lib. 4, ch. 30.

[43] Athanasius, *contra Arianos*, serm. 2.

[44] *In Acta Apostolorum,* Homil. 33.

is consubstantial with the Father, which is a true dogma. Papist is deduced from Pope [Papa], such was even Peter, and Christ himself, as is known. Roman, however, and Romanist, even before 1100 years was the same, which is Catholic, as is clear from St. Ambrose.[45] Add what Chyrostom said in the same sermon quoted above, that it is not bad to be called Catholics by those who govern the Church in the name of Christ, as long as we are not to be called after some man, as the heretics are. It seems as though he foresaw we would be called Papists at some time. Add that we are not called Papists, except by the Lutherans in Germany, and in neighboring regions; we are not however called that in Greece, Asia, Africa, India, and at length, there is no need to mention Italy and Spain.

---

[45] *In oratione de obitu Satyri.*

CHAPTER V
The Second Mark

THE SECOND MARK is Antiquity; for without a doubt the true Church is more ancient than a false one, just as God existed before the devil. We read in the Gospel that the first sowing was good seed, afterwards came the cockle.[46] Also, the Church is called Catholic, because it was in every time, and likewise is called apostolic, because it was founded by the apostles, and hence is the most ancient. That our Church is older than all the associations of pagans, nay more, that our Scripture is older than the gods of the nations, Tertullian proves in his *Apologeticus*.[47]

In every manifest change of religion, these six signs of it are always able to be shown. Firstly, the author of the change. Secondly, some new doctrine. Thirdly, the time in which it began. Fourthly, the place where it began. Fifthly, who opposed it. Sixthly, that some scanty body little by little began to grow when others entered into it. On the other hand, we find all these things in the very Church of Christ, which, nevertheless, was not a new Church, but only a type of change of the status of the Church according to the predictions of the prophets.

First, we know the author was Christ, whereby we are called Christians. Secondly, the new doctrines of the Trinity and Incarnation began to be believed explicitly. Thirdly, this was preached in the 15th year of the Emperor Tiberius Caesar. Fourthly, it began in Judea. Fifthly, this religion was soon assaulted by the scribes and pharisees, and thereafter by the nations with great force. Sixthly we know, in the beginning there were many fewer Christians than there were Jews, even when the separation was made. If, therefore, in this change of the state of the same Church those six things can be shown, the same things can be shown much more in any perfect change. We have already shown all those in the individual sects of heretics. But our adversaries could not show anything like this ever happened in our Church after apostolic times.

We will illustrate the matter with some examples. We know that the author of the Arians was a certain priest from Alexandria named Arius. Likewise,

---

[46] Matthew XIII.

[47] *Apologeticus*, ch. 19 and 20. Cf. St. Augustine, *de Civitate Dei*, bk 18, ch. 37 and 38.

Nestorius, the bishop of Constantinople, was the author of the Nestorians, and moreover, Martin Luther, a priest and Augustinian monk, was the author of the Lutherans.

Secondly, we know what doctrines they invented. Arius taught the Son of God was a mere creature. Nestorius, that in Christ there were two persons. Luther, that men are justified through individual faith alone, that is, men should hold that they are justified through this alone. In like manner, he also denied the Eucharist to be a sacrifice.

Thirdly, we know the times in which they began. The Arian heresy began in the year 324, the Nestorian heresy in 431, and that of the Lutherans in 1517.

Fourthly, we know the places. Arianism began in Egypt, Nestorianism began in Thrace and Lutheranism in Saxony.

Fifthly, we know that right away the Arians were attacked by Pope Sylvester, by the Council of Nicaea, by Sts. Athanasius and Hilary, and others. The Nestorian heresy was attacked by Pope Celestine, the Council of Ephesus, St. Cyril, and many others. The Lutheran heresy was attacked by Pope Leo X, by the Council of Trent, by all Catholic universities and many Theologians.

Sixthly, we know that at the beginnings of these heresies their followers were very few, and from the beginning of their separation there were many more Catholics diffused throughout the world than there were Arians, Nestorians, or even Lutherans, which not even they can deny.

On the other hand, they are unable to show any of these characteristics on our side. For in the first place, they never object to us that there is an author of our sect, nor do they call us by any particular man's name, because if that were the case they would do so with great pleasure.

Secondly, they have never shown the first origin of any of our teachings; in fact, the Centuriators recorded who the authors were that defended our teachings, which they now oppose, but they did not discover the origin, unless it was in the time of the apostles.[48] They even number Justin and Irenaeus among our supporters, whom it is certain followed right after the times of the apostles. In the next chapter of the same citation, they enumerate all the heresies of every age as well as who resisted them, yet, they never record that some heresy was devised by Roman Pontiffs, rather that all heresies were condemned by them. Today, they object to many heresies on our side. Tilman Hesch wrote a book on six hundred heresies of the Popes, but these heresies, apart from the falsehoods of Tilman, are very ancient dogmas, which actually

---

[48] *In singulis Centuriis,* ch. 4, about the end.

can be proved by the Centuriators rather easily. For example, Illyricus discovered our doctrines in every book of the Fathers; but among the Fathers he calls them blemishes, among us, heresies. This is clever on the part of our adversaries: in order to show that we are outside the Church, they call our doctrines heresies, but lest they might appear to be separated from the Church of the Fathers, they call the same doctrine merely "blemishes" when it is found amongst them.

Thirdly, they have never been able to trace out a clear point of our supposed defection from the Church. They simply say that after the first five hundred years this sect began to strengthen, yet when it began, they have absolutely never said.

Fourthly, they never showed, in what place it began, for after the first five hundred years, Pope St. Gregory flourished, with whom the whole world communicated, as can be seen from the epistles which he sent to every land. Likewise, after the death of Gregory the sixth Ecumenical Council was celebrated, wherein one may clearly see, that the whole east and west were joined at that time with the Roman Pontiff as members with their head.

Fifthly, they never showed who attacked it, as though it recently arose, and what councils were convened against it. Indeed, they do object that the Council of Constantinople under Copronymus (which seemed to them to be a general council), condemned images, something that Rome defended. But that was not a general council, since it did not have any true Patriarch. Moreover, that council did **not** condemn a dogma which arose at that time, but an ancient dogma, and one received in the whole Church. It did not establish that the veneration of images should not be received, but rather that it should be abolished, and that images should be stripped from the Basilica. See the works of Cedrenus, Zonaras, and Paul the Deacon.

Sixthly, it cannot in any way be shown that our Church ever separated itself from some greater part, so that those adhering to the Roman See were very few, and the remaining Christians many more; for, from the epistles of St. Gregory, which he wrote to the bishops of the East, as well as to the bishops of Africa, Spain, Gaul, and Italy, it is certain that nearly all Christians communicated with him.

The older Fathers always used this argument from antiquity against heretics to show the true Church. Tertullian says to them: "Who are you, and where do you come from? Where have you been hiding for so long?"[49] Optatus says:

---

[49] *De prescript. Contra haereticos.*

"Show the origin of your seat, you who wish to claim you are the holy Church."[50] St. Hilary in his work on the Trinity: "It seems to me these latest times bring propagators of blasphemy. It is too late for these unheard of teachings to correct my faith, which I received from you and in which I have put my trust, O Lord."[51] St. Jerome says: "Whoever you are that assert new doctrines, I ask you, that you spare Roman ears, that you spare the faith, which has been praised by the apostolic mouth. Why after four hundred years do you strive to teach what we did not know before? Even to this day, the Christian was clean without that doctrine of yours."[52] He adds at the end of his work against the Luciferians: "In this very matter, because they were established later, they show themselves to be of the sort that the Apostle predicted were going to come about." Thereupon, St. Augustine, places antiquity among the marks of the Church.[53]

Our adversaries bring four arguments to these answers. Firstly, Calvin responds that no unconquerable argument can be produced from antiquity. For Ishmael was older than Isaac, and nevertheless it was said: "Cast out the maidservant, and her son." But Ishmael was not a figure of a false religion, but only that the Old Testament was good and from God. Also, since the state of men in that Covenant was of servants who are spoken of with respect to fear, a new and more perfect Covenant ought to succeed it, which pertains to the free, who are lead by love. The Apostle writes in Galatians: "It has been written, that Abraham had two sons . . . who are spoken of in allegory: these are the two Testaments, etc."[54]

Secondly they say our Church can not be shown to have begun in some time or through some author, etc., because it is not really new, but because it happened together with that change and little by little error crept in and was not averted and while the shepherds were sleeping. Whereas, while certainly some changes did not happen all together, but little by little, as is clear from Luther, who in the beginning did not deny indulgences, etc., nevertheless, we

---

[50] Optatus, lib. 2 *contra Parmenianum.*

[51] Hilary, *De Trinitate*, bk 6.

[52] Jerome, *in Epistol. Ad Pammachium et Oceanum.*

[53] *Contra epist. Fundamenti*, ch. 4.

[54] *Instit.*, Bk 4, ch. 2 § 3.

do know about individuals, when and how they arose. On that account, the Gospel of Matthew does not say the cockle arose while the men were sleeping, but was sown *while* they were sleeping; it soon appeared, however, and was recognized. How then were our "heresies" not detected for a thousand years? Certainly, not only the shepherds, but even God would have slept too long, if through so many ages he never roused anyone, who would resist these errors. And it would have made a lie of what we read in the Gospel: "I am with you always, even to the consummation of the age."

Thirdly they say that although it cannot be shown when the beginning of this depravity occurred, that it can be shown when the eminent change occurred. For in the beginning of the year 600, the Pope obviously was changed into Antichrist, when the Roman pontiff obtained from Phocas the emperor, that he should be called head of bishops, and when he opened the temple of the Pantheon of all the gods. The Centuriators of Magdeburg teach this, and many of our adversaries agree. Theodore Bibliander also, in the tablets of his Chronology in the beginning of the year 600, placed the appearance of Antichrist, that is of the Pope, and Luther, by a computation of time, preferred St. Gregory as the last pope; and here and there the Calvinists and Lutherans extend the purity of the Church to the first 500 or 600 years.

But in the first place, after the year 670, long after the times of Phocas, the sixth Ecumenical Council was celebrated (which our adversaries receive as sacrosanct as is clear both from the confession of Zurich, and the Centuriators, as well as others). In that very Council the party of the Roman Pope Agatho was preeminent, for his teaching was explicated through legates and through his epistles, and everyone followed them, as even the Centuriators amply relate.[55] Either the Pope was not yet Antichrist, or the whole Church, and a holy general council both venerated and followed Antichrist.

On that account, it is false that Phocas first gave the name of head of the Church to the Roman Pontiff, because Justinian the elder, who was almost a hundred years before Phocas, in his epistle to Pope John II, calls that Pope head of all Churches with eloquent words. And this same thing is found in an epistle of the same John II responding to Justinian, where the Pope repeats a summary of the letter of the Emperor, and it is found on each side of the Epistle.[56] The Centuriators are not ignorant of this, for they recall the fourth law of the Codex,

---

[55] *Cent.* 7, ch. 9.

[56] *In codice*, bk. 1, titul 1, leg. 4, and 6.

which was taken up from the letter of Pope John.[57] Therefore they lie against their own joint knowledge.

Also, before the times of Justinian, the Council of Chalcedon calls Pope Leo the head of all Churches. Even Leo himself thus addresses Rome: "Through the holy seat of Blessed Peter, made head of the world and more extensively, a guardian in divine religion rather than earthly dominion."[58] And further down: "It is no small thing that, what bellicose labor supplied to you, is what Christian peace has placed under you." Therefore, Phocas was *not* the first who gave this name to the Roman Pontiff, but the first to restrain the pride of the bishop of Constantinople, who wanted to be made equal with the Roman Pontiff.

Now, concerning the Church, which is called the Pantheon: I say firstly that it is an argument against our adversaries. For, we read in Daniel, that Antichrist will fight against all gods, and alone in secret would adore the god Maozim, and in 2 Thessalonians it is said he will be elevated above every other, which is called God. Therefore, if the Pope opened a temple to all the gods, in such a matter he would not be Antichrist. Besides, long before the temple of the Pantheon was consecrated to God in memory of all the saints, there already were temples in Rome were consecrated to St. Peter, Paul, Lawrence and Sebastian, etc.

But Melanchthon objects that the invocation of the saints did not exist before the times of St. Gregory,[59] therefore it began then. I respond: it is a lie. For many Fathers, and among them Ambrose, called to mind the invocation of the saints.[60] On Antichrist, however and the invocation of the saints we have already treated upon it in many other places.[61]

Fourthly, Calvin responds in the preface of the Institutes, that his Church is not new, but very ancient; more so, it is the very Church which Christ founded, however, it was not seen through many ages, and now at length has appeared. But St. Augustine makes an argument against this same opinion which

---

[57] *Cent. 6*, ch. 10, col. 670.

[58] Leo, *Serm. 1 de sanctis Petro et Paulo.*

[59] *In Confesione et Apolog.* Art. 21.

[60] Lib. *De viduis.*

[61] See *De Romano Pontifice*, bk 5.

previously was held by the Donatists;[62] either that [his] Church, which appears today, perished before and now has been resurrected; or it did not perish but had only been hidden, and now has raised its head. The first proposition cannot be, for it could not then be reborn if the mother had perished. If it perished, St. Augustine asks, "Therefore from where did the Donatists appear? From what soil did it blossom? From what sea did it emerge? From what heaven did it fall?" Besides, the promises of Christ would be false: "The gates of hell will not prevail against it." And in the last chapter of Matthew: "I am with you, even to the consummation of the age."[63] The second proposition cannot be, because then either that hidden Church professed its faith, or it did not profess it; if it professed, therefore it was not hidden, but manifest: and if manifest, how could nobody notice it? Why wasn't it taken and coerced by inquisitors, who already arose in the Church a long time before Luther? Why is there no vestige, no memory of them? If they did not profess the faith, but truly and properly hid (which the other side is compelled to defend), therefore that was not the Church, and hence there was no true Church in the world. For, as they say, the confession of faith is a mark of the true Church: and "Confession by mouth is made unto salvation."[64]

For that reason, if that were the case, how, when Luther and Calvin appeared, was there nobody who would have united themselves to them, except for those who were deceived by them? If many Lutherans and Calvinists were so hidden, wouldn't many have soon recognized in the preaching of Luther and Calvin their friends, and even though they were not called, run to them? It was not so; for nearly everybody who is a Lutheran or Calvinist, affirms themselves to have been Catholic beforehand, and did not think that Catholicism was a new doctrine. Moreover, Luther himself affirms that he at some point was not Lutheran, but a Catholic monk, and celebrated masses for 15 years seriously and devoutly.[65]

In the end, if the Church was so hidden as Calvin says, then it would follow that the Church of Christ was worse and more miserable than every heretical

---

[62] Augustine, *against the Donatists*, bk 3; *De Baptismo*, ch. 2.

[63] Matthew XVI: 19; XXVIII.

[64] Romans X.

[65] See the book, *De Missa angulari*, or Joannes Cochlaeus, *in actis Lutheri* for the year 1534. Likewise, bk 2 of Luther against Zwingli, or *Septicipitem* of John Cochlaeus, ch. 24.

sect, and in that even worse off than the Jewish people after the destruction of Jerusalem, which certainly is a blasphemy, although God everywhere predicted the glory of the Church through the prophets, and promised that he would be with it always. What follows then, is obvious; for every heretical sect has its temples, its bishops, its sacraments. And in like manner, the Jews after the destruction of Jerusalem always had some synagogues, where they freely exercised their ceremonies, as can be seen in the times of Pope St. Gregory,[66] and they were never compelled to worship false gods. Yet, the Church which Calvin imagines was hiding for nearly a thousand years, had no temples, no sacred rites, no bishops, it did not even have a corner of earth where it could freely exercise acts of its religion, and what is worse, was compelled to be in servitude to false gods, to adore idols, to communicate in sacrileges, which is an even more horrible and longer captivity, than there ever was among the Jews; moreover, that Church of his would be even more deformed than the ruins of the synagogue.

---

[66] Bk 7, epist. 5.

CHAPTER VI
The Third Mark

HE THIRD MARK is Long Duration, without interruption. Truly the Church is called Catholic, not only because it always was, but even because it always will be, according to Daniel IX: "The kingdom which will not be destroyed in eternity." Also Acts V: "If this is a work or council of men, it will come to nothing; but if it is from God, you cannot destroy it." Concerning the heretics, however, St. Paul says: "They will proceed no further."[67] St. Cyprian says that schismatics always swarm in the beginning, but cannot have increase, rather immediately fade out due to their deprave rivalry.[68] St. Augustine, commenting on Psalm 57, where it is read "they come to nothing, as water flowing down," says: "Let them not terrify you, brethren, as certain rivers which are spoken of as running streams. They are filled with the waters of winter. Do not fear: after a while it passes, the water runs down, it resounds for a time, soon it will cease. They cannot stand for a long time. Many difficulties have already died off, they ran in their streams as much as they could, they flowed down: they are dry streams, scarcely a memory of them is found to show that they ever were."

Now it is certain that our Church has endured to this point from the beginning of the world. Or, if we speak from the status of the New Testament, it has endured from Christ to this point for 1577 years, in vain have all attacked her, first the Jews, then the pagans, lastly the heretics. Not only has it endured, but even has increased from persecutions. As the waters of floods rush over the palaces of kings, and also overthrow them, so have persecutions destroyed temporal kingdoms, but the kingdom of Christ, which is the Church, not only did they not destroy, but made even more glorious. Therefore St. Justin Martyr says in his Dialogue with Trypho, that persecution is to the Church, like pruning is to vineyards, as indeed by the pruning of vineyards they are called to fruitfulness, so also the Church rises in persecutions. Tertullian elegantly calls the blood of the martyrs the seed of Christians[69], which Pope Leo seems to have

---

[67] 2 Tim. III: 9.

[68] Cyprian, *Epistol. 2.*

[69] *Apologeticus,* last chapter.

expressed when he said: "The Church by persecutions is not decreased, but increased, and the Lord's field is always clothed with the richest grain, while from a grain which falls individually, many more are born."[70]

However much the heretics of this time do not concede that our Church has endured for 1577 years, yet they concede it to have endured without any interruption from St. Gregory the great to this time; that is nearly a thousand years. Such a time even by itself, would still be longer than the life of any heresy; certainly they cannot show through any history or ancient writing that a change of religion came to pass in the Roman Church in the time of St. Gregory.

Thereupon, it can be proven that our Church is the true Church even by this argument; for before the times of Luther, there were no other religions in the world but these; Paganism, Judaism, Islam, Greek Orthodoxy, Nestorianism, the heresy of the Hussites and the Roman Church. Now it is certain that the true Church of Christ was not with any of the aforementioned sects, as even the Lutherans will affirm, therefore it was the Roman Church, what follows from their opinion is that every true and visible Church perished from the world—which cannot be, as we taught above. But on the other hand, all heretical sects fail after a time, apart from those which have recently arisen.

Theodoret relates that seventy six different heresies which had arisen were present even in his time, and witnesses that they all had been extinguished, with the exception of a very few.[71] St. Augustine counts eighty eight heresies, wherein he witnesses that many perished.[72] We count even to the time of Luther two hundred diverse families of heretics: but from these none survive, except a certain relic of the Nestorians and Monophysites in the east as well as the Hussites in Bohemia; all the rest have utterly perished. And the providence of God is exceedingly wonderful in this matter, because hitherto even to the times of Luther, there were at least two hundred heresiarchs, of which many had several bishops, Churches, and powerful patrons, even emperors and kings. They wrote so many numerous books, that it appeared they would never die out; and nevertheless they did, so that none of them survived, not even their books, nor dogmas, nor names, or any vestige, except in the books of Catholics. Therefore, if Catholics had not written their names in their books, we would not

---

[70] *Serm. 1* de Petro et Paulo.

[71] Theodoret, *de haereticis fabulis*, bk 3.

[72] *De haeresibus*;; *Expositiones in psalmos*, 57.

know that they ever existed.

How strong did the roots upon which the Arian heresy rested appear to be in the times of St. Athanasius and Hilary? But now, I ask, where is it? It vanished as dust, which is scattered by the winds of the earth. Two hundred years ago the Albigensian heresy reigned in France, which apart from force of doctrine, abounded more in soldiers and power than the heresy of the Calvinists now, as can be recognized from Paulus Aemilius:[73] and nevertheless, where are the Albigensians now? How few are they who have heard or named them?

Next, the Lutherans were scarcely born when they began to wither, the reign of Luther began in 1517, but he reigned for scarcely seven years, for in 1525 Zwingli arose, and two years later the Anabaptists rose, who drew the greater part of the Lutherans away from Luther and to themselves. Yet the Lutherans who remain so changed the doctrine of Luther, that hardly any pure Lutherans can be found. Illyricus seriously complains about that in the prefaces of all the Centuries.

But Zwingli did not reign long, for in 1538 Calvin arose, who strengthened in such a short time, that scarcely a few towns in Switzerland remained Zwinglian. In the same manner the Calvinists were reduced by the Libertines in France, the Trinitarians in Poland, and the Samosatens in Transylvania, daily they are made fewer and fewer.

Calvin, as he was perceptive, foresaw that his reign would not last long, and predicted in the preface of the Geneva Catechism, which he sent to his ministers in eastern Frisia: "I am anxious about posterity, that still I can hardly dare to think about it. Unless God should miraculously bring aid from heaven, I myself see the worst barbarism to threaten the world. And would that our sons would understand, that this is more a true prophecy than conjecture." Such anxiety of Calvin sufficiently declares his sect to be plainly a human affair, not devised by the Spirit of God, but by a certain industry and human plan, and therefore by far is missing that spirit, which said: "Upon this rock I will build my Church, and the gates of hell will not prevail against it."

The Centuriators also prophesy the same thing in the preface of the second century concerning their Lutheranism: "Especially variations in doctrine and inclinations seem to threaten it; and thus the sins of men earn such atrocities which happen day after day. And indeed, the times of the German prophet Martin Luther, by whose voice and ministry the light of the Gospel was recalled as from Egyptian darkness, just about corresponded to the age of the apostles.

---

[73] *De rebus Gallorum*, bk 6.

Now, however, it has been taken away, as we enter another age of the gospel, where many fanatics begin to sprout, and rule little by little." Later, in the preface to the fifth Century, after they showed the particular articles on free will, on justifying faith, and on good works, they declare that they are not fully defended by many Lutherans, but subjected to Papism: "That truth recently made so clear has perished. Philosophy, Papism and other sects far and wide occupy the first seat in the temple of God."

Therefore we conclude with St. Jerome, in the last dialogue against the Luciferians: "I advance the brief and open opinion of my mind, that I must remain in that Church, which was founded by the apostles, and endures even to this day." And with St. Augustine: "Will we hesitate to submit to the bosom of that Church, which obtained the summit of authority by the apostolic seat through successions of bishops, while the heretics roared around in vain?"[74]

---

[74] *De Utilitate Credendi*, ch. 17.

CHAPTER VII
The Fourth Mark

THE FOURTH mark is the Extent, or the Multitude and Diversity of Believers. Indeed, a Church that is truly Catholic ought not only to embrace all times but all places, all nations and all races of men. Therefore, St. Vincent of Lérin explains what a Catholic might be in his *Commonitorium*, where he says that they are properly Catholics, who hold to that which has been believed always, everywhere and by all. And thus it was preached in the Psalms: "I will give to you the nations as your inheritance, and as your possession the ends of the earth,"[75] and, "Your dominion will be from sea to sea."[76] And the Lord himself in both the last chapter of Luke and the first of Acts of the apostles, says that the Gospel must be preached in all nations, which was begun in Jerusalem.

However, some things must be observed before we shall draw out the argument on this Mark. The first is from St. Augustine and St. Bede, namely, that for the Church to be Catholic, first it is required that it should not exclude any times, places, or races of men; whereby it is distinguished from the Synagogue, which was a particular Church, not a catholic one, because it was bound to one time, that is, even to the coming of the Messiah; likewise, in one place, that is the temple of Solomon, outside of which they could not sacrifice, and to one family, that is the sons of Jacob.[77]

Secondly, as noted by St. Augustine,[78] that the Church might be catholic, it is not required that it must be in every place of the world, but merely that it becomes conspicuous in all provinces, and bears fruit in them, so that in all provinces someone should be from the Church; until this should happen, the day of the Lord will not come, as obviously is predicted in Matthew XXIV.

---

[75] Psalm II.

[76] Psalm LXXI.

[77] Augustine, *de unitate Ecclesiae*, ch. 6; Bede *in Cant.*, ch. 6.

[78] *Epistol. 80 ad Hesychium.*

Thirdly from Driedo,[79] it is not required that in this it happens together so that in one time there ought to necessarily be some faithful in all lands; it is sufficient enough if it happens successively. Whereby it follows that if only one land should retain the true faith, still truly and properly it could be called the Catholic Church, provided that it should be clearly shown that it was one and the same with that which was in some time or at different times in the whole world, in so far as now whichever diocese you like is called Catholic, because it has continued with others, which make the one Church catholic.

But you will say, "this is to fall into the error of Petilianus and the Donatists, who said the Church was in the whole world, but afterward perished from all provinces, and remained only in Africa, whom St. Augustine condemned."[80] I respond, the Donatists erred in two things. First, they wanted the Church to only be in Africa while at the same time it manifestly still bore fruit in the whole world. Secondly, because their African Church would not continue with those which were in the whole world because in those were always found the good and the wicked, as St. Augustine proves, and the Donatists wanted only the good.

Lastly, with respect to this mark, although the Church ought not necessarily be in all places at the same time, nevertheless in this time it ought necessarily be, or have been, in a greater part of the world. For, everyone agrees, even the heretics, that the Church is already old; if therefore it would not have increased in its adolescence and youth, how could it rise now in old age? It would behoove it, therefore, to have already increased, and also if not occupied the whole world, at least a great part of it.

Now, that our Church occupies a great part of the world, and is truly Catholic is so proved. For in the time of the apostles it began to bear fruit in the whole world, as Paul says.[81] Likewise, in the time of Irenaeus, it was scattered through the whole world, that is, through all provinces then known, which he relates.[82] Tertullian reports the same thing later in his time,[83] as does St.

---

[79] Driedo, *de Ecclesia dogmat.* Nota, bk 4, ch. 2, par. 2.

[80] *Sermon 2 on Psalm 101.*

[81] Colossians I.

[82] Irenaeus, bk 1, ch. 3.

[83] *Contra Judaeos*, ch. 3.

Cyprian.[84] St. Athanasius says the same thing in his book on the humanity of the word, and a little after, Sts. John Chrysostom and Jerome,[85] St. Augustine as well as Theodoret,[86] and Pope St. Leo the Great.[87] Moreover, St. Prosper of Aquitaine sings thus:

> Rome the seat of Peter, for pastoral honor,
> Made head for the world, whatever it does not possess by arms,
> It holds by religion.[88]

Perhaps, in fact, our adversaries do not deny these things. We will show the same thing from later times. It is plain that in the time of St. Gregory, our Church was spread throughout the whole world as we recorded above from the same letter of St. Gregory to the Churches of the east, as well as of Africa, Spain, France, England and Sicily. Likewise, from Bede, and indeed St. Bernard who, disputing in the presence of King Roger of Sicily, asserted in his time that the whole east and west obeyed the Roman Pontiff, and in like manner France, Germany, England, Iberia, and many barbarian nations.[89]

Thereafter, in our time, the Roman Church apart from Italy and all of Spain, apart from nearly all of France, Germany, England, Poland, Bohemia, Hungary, Greece, Syria, Ethiopia and Egypt, in which many Catholics are found, in the new world itself, we have Churches without the mingling of heretics, in all four parts of the world; to the east, in the Indies, to the west, in America; to the north in Japan; to the south in Brazil, and in the further part of Africa. But the sects of the heretics have never occupied the new world, or at least, only a scanty part

---

[84] *De unitate Ecclesiae.*

[85] In Matt. Ch. 24.

[86] Augustine, *Epist. 78 and 80 ad Hesychium*; Theodoret, *De Legibus.*

[87] *Serm. 1 de sanctis Petro et Paulo.*

[88] Lib. *De ingratis.*

[89] See *The life of St. Barnard*, bk 2, ch. 7.

of it.[90]

The sects of Islam, along with the heresies of Nestorius and the Monophysites, which still flourish in the east, never passed over to the west. The Lutheran Heretics have never crossed the sea, nor seen Asia, Africa, Egypt or Greece. Wherein we understand that what is found in the beginning of the preface on the Concord of the Lutherans, published in 1580, is a lie, where they say that the Augsburg confession has spread throughout the whole world, and has begun to be in the mouth and speech of all. But from three parts of the world, two greater ones, Asia and Africa, the name of this Confession has never been heard. In Europe there are many lands, such as all of Greece, Italy, Spain, who in fact know nothing of the Augsburg confession, let alone exercise it. France, Switzerland and England do not accept it, unless it is in name only; nay more, it is a rare city which is possessed of only one heretical sect. And although it appears at this time that the heretics obtained a great part of the north, nevertheless, all those places are not held by one sect, but many, which fight among themselves no less than with us.

St. Augustine teaches beautifully that, as the Church is everywhere, so also heresy is everywhere. But the Church is one and the same everywhere; heresy, however, is not the same, but very different, which does not know one from the other, and hence none of them can be Catholic. While the Church, meanwhile, as a living vine, extends its palms everywhere.[91]

The heretics cannot hope that their sect should at some time in the future occupy the whole world: for the Church ought not to begin to rise when it has already grown old, as we said above. And if St. Augustine found it most absurd, that the heresy of the Donatists should be propagated after the year 300 into the whole world,[92] how much more absurd will it be now after the year 1577? Will the Lutheran or Calvinist heresy really be diffused from Wittenberg into the whole world?

---

[90] In 1590, the English alone had small settlements in America, which paled in comparison to the Spanish and Portugese. The first large colony of Protestants would not appear until the 17th century, consisting only of the English and the Dutch. -Translator's note.

[91] *De pastor.* Ch. 8; *Contra epist. Fundamenti*, ch. 4; *De utilitate credendi*, ch. 14, 17 and other places.

[92] *De unitate Ecclesiae*, ch. 14 and 15.

CHAPTER VIII
The Fifth Mark

HE FIFTH Mark is the Succession of Bishops in the Roman Church deduced from the apostles even to us; hence it is called Apostolic. Besides, all the Fathers used this succession as a most clear argument to show the true Church. Irenaeus enumerates the roman bishops from Peter, even to Eleutherius, who sat in his times. And he says that, through this succession all heretics are confounded.[93] Tertullian says: "Let the heretics start from the origins of their Churches, let them unfold the order of their bishops, so through the succession running down from the beginning, their first bishop had someone from the apostles, or apostolic men as his author and predecessor. In this manner, the Church of the Romans relates that Clement was ordained by Peter."[94]

The heretics sometimes fabricated such a thing. Eusebius in his history and in the Chronicle, as well as Jerome and Prosper who continued the Chronicle of Eusebius, diligently recorded the succession of roman bishops, so that the continuation of the Church would be manifest. Epiphanius enumerates in order the roman bishops, and adds: "Nobody should marvel that we have reviewed individuals so exactly. Through this, indeed, clarity is shown."[95]

Optatus enumerates all the roman bishops from Peter even to Syricius, who sat in the seat of Peter at that time, in order that he might show that the Donatists did not have a Church who could not embark on a like succession back to the apostles: "You, show the origin of your seat, who would claim the holy Church for yourselves."[96]

Next, St. Augustine enumerates for the same purpose, the roman pontiffs from Peter even to Anastasius, who sat at that time. And against the position of Donatus he says: "Count the priests, or, from the seat of Peter itself, and in that

[93] Irenaeus bk 3. ch. 3.

[94] *De praescript.*

[95] Epiphanius, *Haeres..*, 27.

[96] *Contra Parmenianum*, bk 2.

order, of the Fathers who succeeded him. Look to it, he is the rock, which the proud gates of hell shall not conquer."[97] And again: "Keep me in the Church which is from that seat of Peter the Apostle, whom the Lord entrusted with the task of feeding his sheep, in a succession of priests even to the present episcopacy."[98]

If, therefore, so many Fathers took pains to show that the Church is true by the continuation of 12, or 20, or 40 Popes, how much more should we mark an uninterrupted continuation of 200 or more Popes? Especially when we shall see that other apostolic sees fell away, such as Antioch, Alexandria, and Jerusalem, whereby, after these places were stolen from the [eastern] Romans by the Persians or Saracens, which happened nine hundred years ago, there succession either ceased, or was very obscure. And in regard to the city of Rome, whose ownership has so often changed between rulers, at one time in the hands of the emperors, then the Gothic kings, then Greek Exarchs, then even consuls, whether justly or unjustly in their power, and as often as this city has been turned over, nevertheless the seat of Peter has never failed, never been overturned, but has always remained immovable.

In the event you should wish to better understand this argument, some things must be noted. First, in no way can the Church exist without shepherds and bishops, as St. Cyprian rightly teaches, the Church is the people united to the bishop, and the bishop is in the Church, and the Church in the bishop.[99] For that reason St. Jerome says: "If it does not have priests it is not a Church."[100] This is certainly proved from St. Paul: "And he gave some as apostles, some, however, as prophets, others shepherds and teachers to the consummation of the saints, to build up the body of Christ, until we might all meet, etc."[101] Where he teaches apostles, he means the pastors who were going to exist in the Church even to the day of judgment. Then indeed, we will meet the Lord in the unity of faith, in the perfect man, in the measure of the age of plenitude of Christ. The same apostle teaches that bishops are the shepherds of the flock, in Acts XX:

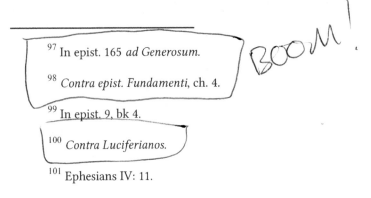

[97] In epist. 165 *ad Generosum.*

[98] *Contra epist. Fundamenti*, ch. 4.

[99] In epist. 9, bk 4.

[100] *Contra Luciferianos.*

[101] Ephesians IV: 11.

"Attend to your own and the whole flock, in which the Holy Spirit has placed you as bishops to rule the Church of God." Furthermore, even Luther does not deny it, in fact he preferably places among the marks of the Church to have true shepherds.[102] From which it follows, it is not a true Church that has either no shepherds, or at least no true ones.

The second note; only those who are within the Church have always been held to be true bishops. That is, those who were shown to descend from the apostles through a legitimate succession and ordination. All others were thieves and robbers, obviously who did not enter through the gate, but went in from another place. For it is certain that Christ, by whom the Church of the new Testament began, only chose twelve apostles as bishops and priests, and entrusted to them all authority of shepherding and governing the Church; but the apostles afterwards chose and ordained other bishops, and handed to them the same power, who thereupon ordained others. This is shown, not only by ancient historians like Eusebius and others, but even by the Centuriators of Magdeburg. Hence, because Paul, who was made an apostle outside of that order by Christ after his ascension into heaven, was not recognized in the Church for such, unless first he would have been baptized into the Church and was received in friendship by the apostles; nay more, he was ordained by them, as is clear from the Scripture.[103] Thus, among the people of the Old Testament, who were propagated by carnal generation, none could be counted as among that people of God, unless he descended from the twelve sons of Jacob; moreover none were priests, unless they descended from Levi through Aaron. Therefore, they very diligently conserved genealogies, as is seen in the entire Old Testament. In the same way, among the people of the New Testament, they are multiplied by spiritual generation, so that none are Christians, except converted through the apostles, or their successors, or those sent by them; none are bishops, unless they succeed legitimately to the same, and therefore we so diligently record the successions of bishops.

The third note requires two things; that some bishop should rightly be said to descend from the apostles, and hence be a legitimate bishop. One is succession, the other is ordination. As to succession, it requires that he who desires to be counted as a true bishop should succeed some apostle, in the way that Clement succeeded Peter, and Polycarp succeeded John. Certainly he should succeed someone whom an apostle made a bishop, as Ignatius succeeded

---

[102] Luther, *de Ecclesia et Conciliis.*

[103] Acts IX and XIII; Galatians I.

Evodius and Anianus, Mark whom Peter had made bishops, or at length, if the episcopacy is new, that he becomes a bishop by one who has apostolic authority, which is the Roman Pontiff alone. St. Augustine writes that in the Roman Church the supremacy of the apostolic seat always flourishes.[104]

The reasoning behind this, is that the establishment of new episcopacies cannot pertain to anyone who might have a defined region, such as particular bishops, but to he who is over the whole Church, and to whom properly falls the care of propagating the Church, such as were all the apostles. Indeed, Peter did so by his office, and the rest by delegation, and whoever enters otherwise is not of the apostolic Church, since he cannot show his origin from the apostles. Nevertheless, we do not deny whether even patriarchs and metropolitans could at sometime erect new episcopacies, which St. Athanasius certainly did in the east, and St. Boniface had done in Germany; yet they had the faculty from the apostolic seat.

As far as ordination, it is required that for one to be a bishop, he was ordained by three bishops, who even themselves were ordained by others, and these by others, until one should arrive at the apostles. This is clearly held in canon 1 of the Apostolic Canons, where it is commanded that a bishop should be ordained by two or three bishops, that is by two assisting the metropolitan, or by many.[105] Likewise, Anacletus teaches that James was ordained a bishop at Jerusalem by Peter, James and John, and in the same manner by three at the least, all others ought to be ordained."[106] The same is held in the Council of Nicaea and Carthage.[107] Nay more, the Apostle indicates this very thing when he writes: "Do not forget the grace which is in you, which was given to you with the imposition of hands of the priests."[108] Accordingly, by the name of priests [πρεσβυτεροι] he understands the body of bishops, who together with the ordinand placed their hands above the head of the one to be ordained, as St. John Chrysostom, Theopylactus and Oecumenius express. And it is no wonder

---

[104] *Epist. 162.*

[105] The Apostolic Canons are decrees found in the Eighth book of the *Apostolic Constitutions*, which date from the early Church, although modern scholarship questions whether it was written by the Apostles. -Translator's note.

[106] *Epist. 2.*

[107] *Nicaea, I.*, ch. 4; *Carthage* IV, ch. 2.

[108] 1 Timothy IV.

that the body of bishops is called a body "of priests", for the noun *presbyterus* formerly was synonymous with bishops [επισκοπος] as is certain from the epistle of Irenaeus to Pope Victor, which is found in Eusebius.[109] In that epistle, Irenaeus addresses popes as roman priests [*presbyteros*], namely Victor, Anicetus, Pius, Telesphorus, and Xystus. Therefore, there can be no doubt whether it was ordinary for at least three bishops to be required to ordain a new bishop, unless perhaps by some dispensation with one bishop ordaining while abbots were invested with episcopal insignia, who in turn functioned in the place of bishops, as was usually done at some time due to the lack of bishops.

The fourth note: it was the custom of the ancient heretics to imitate many Churches in the ordination of bishops, as we see from St. Cyprian and Augustine. Therefore, the holy Fathers did not reprove them for that reason, rather they did so because there was a defect of succession, and from that alone proved that they were not true bishops, seeing that they did not pertain to the apostolic Church, since they did not have their origin through succession from the apostles. Now, the heretics of our times have neither, that is, neither ordination, nor succession, and on that account are by far more shameless than any other heretics ever were, who usurped for themselves the name and office of bishop.

From that the unanswerable argument is taken up in this way: The Church cannot be without bishops, as we have shown. There are not bishops among the Lutherans, for they do not have ordination, nor succession from the apostles: therefore, the Church is not among them. And indeed, neither Luther, who is held as the Bishop of Wittenberg, nor Zwingli, who is held as the Bishop of Zurich, nor Oecolampadius, who, on an epitaph on his tomb, is called the first bishop of Basel, nor Calvin who is called the bishop of Geneva, none of them would deny this, since none of them were ordained by three bishops, nor by one with a dispensation with assisting abbots, as has been noted. At any rate, by the Nicene Fathers and the Fathers of the Council of Carthage, nay more, even by the apostles themselves, those who had stated that a bishop ought to be ordained by three other bishops, the aforementioned are not true bishops, and what Cyprian says agrees: "These assume for themselves the name of bishop who put themselves in charge, beyond what one would expect from the rash, putting themselves forward so as to constitute themselves without any law of ordination, being given the episcopacy by no man."[110]

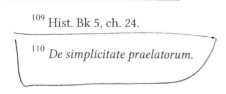

[109] Hist. Bk 5, ch. 24.

[110] *De simplicitate praelatorum.*

39

Now, John of Brenz responds: "We are legitimately called thus by the people and the government, and received the episcopacy from them." Now, we do not dispute on the election of a bishop, which we know was celebrated differently during different times. Indeed, it is certain that the apostles and the old roman bishops sent bishops to different cities without any requisite agreement of the people. It is also certain that at some time the people, together with the clergy, chose the bishop, and at other times, only the clergy. For the rest, no matter how the election happened, ordination was always necessary, which *not* the people, but the bishops alone (and at that at least three) regularly conferred, which no one is ignorant of, except a man who reads nothing. Let Luther say by which bishops he was ordained that he should be made the bishop of Wittenberg. Let the rest say by whom they were ordained, but they do not because they cannot.

Thereupon, because they did not succeed in the episcopacy of ancient bishops, it is absolutely certain that in all cities, where these have made themselves bishops, there were already beforehand, and still are even in many other places, Catholic bishops that had legitimately succeeded older ones; and one does not succeed, unless the bishops have died, or been legitimately deposed. They even claim that they are the first bishops of these cities. Certainly there still exists in Basel, the epitaph on the tomb of Oecolampadius, where it says, as I noted a little before, and I myself have read it, not without a laugh, that Oecolampadius was the first bishop of this city. Concerning these things, therefore, the same thing as what St. Cyprian said in his epistle to Magnus may be recalled: "Novatian is not in the Church, nor can he be counted a bishop, who with contempt for apostolic tradition, succeeded no one and was ordained by himself . . . How can one be considered a shepherd, who as a profane stranger succeeded no one and began from himself while the true shepherd remains, and has succession by ordination in the Church of God, while presiding in that office?"[111] He also adds, in his epistle to Antoninus: "Cornelius was made a bishop when the place of Fabian, that is, the place of Peter, the place of the sacerdotal chair, was empty, in which it had been occupied by the will of God, and also by all of our firm agreement. Therefore, whoever now would wish to be made the bishop, it is necessary that he become a bishop on the outside."[112] Similar things to this were cited above on legitimate succession, from Irenaeus, Tertullian, Epiphanius, Optatus and Augustine.

Yet, they object, that Papist bishops have left the true faith, therefore, they

---

[111] Bk 1, *Epist. 6 ad Magnum.*

[112] Bk 4, *Epist. 2 ad Antonianum.*

are no longer bishops, thus pious ministers can rightly take up their places.

I respond to this argument of Brenz (after which he admits that there may be a doubt where the true faith might be, although with us it is very certain): we cannot depose catholic bishops who have possessed their seats for so many centuries peacefully, unless they are legitimately judged and condemned; for in every controversy the condition of the one possessing it is better. Moreover, it is certain that catholic bishops were not condemned by any legitimate judgment. For who condemned them, apart from the Lutherans? But these are accusers, not judges. Who indeed made them our judges? On that account, even if our bishops were already condemned, they would not immediately succeed them, when no one had made them bishops, that is, those who had the authority of establishing bishops: nor would they be true bishops since no one ordained them, who had the right to ordain as we showed above.

Secondly, the same objection of Brenz, which is in his prolegomena against Pedro de Soto: Caiaphas legitimately succeeded the older priests, and could even deduce his elders from Aaron, and nevertheless the apostles did not seek that they should be ordained by Caiaphas; rather they legitimately succeeded Caiaphas and all those bishops against the will of the latter, and were made bishops and priests without any succession, therefore even the ordinary bishops might imitate Caiaphas, although without their ordination and succession they govern the episcopacy.

I respond: The priesthood of Aaron was temporal, and only endured until the beginning of the New Testament; thereupon, the priesthood according to the order of Melchisedech began, which was established by Christ. Since the apostles were the first fruits of that priesthood, they did not need to succeed Caiaphas, but are the beginning of the new priesthood, as is clear from Psalm CIX: "You are a priest forever;" and from chapter VII of the Hebrews. Therefore, as there were not true priests from Aaron even to Christ, unless they had succeeded Aaron, so from the apostles even to the end of the world there will not be true priests, except for those who succeed the apostles. Nevertheless, it is true that the priests of the Aaronic priesthood should be held in honor unto burial; the apostles honored that, as is clear from St. Cyprian,[113] where he adduces the fact from Acts: "I didn't know brethren, that he is the chief priest."[114]

Thirdly: Calvin objects, asking for what reason should we also enumerate

---

[113] Bk 1 *Epist. 3 ad Cornelium*; bk 4, *Epist. 9 ad Florentium Pupianum.*

[114] Acts XXIII: 5.

the successions of the bishops of Africa, Egypt and all of Asia, and he himself responds by insulting us, because that most holy succession perished there.[115]

I respond: Calvin either wishes to conclude from this that because the succession perished in those places, there is not a Church, or there is a Church. If the first, he argues for us: For if there is not a Church there, because there is no succession, therefore here there is a Church, because here there is a succession. If the second, we respond, those who pertained to the true Church in those places indeed could not show a continual succession of bishops of their particular place, but could show the continual succession of all bishops, who are Roman bishops, to whom these affirmed themselves to be subject. This is the reason why the old bishops were more solicitous about the succession of the Roman Pontiff than they were of their own. Irenaeus was the Bishop of Lyons in Gaul, Optatus and Augustine were bishops in Africa, Epiphanius of Salamis in Cypris, Eusebius of Caesarea in Palestine, and nevertheless, none of them wanted to elaborate the succession of their Church, but only of the Roman Church. Indeed, it appeared sufficient for them to show the continual succession in the principle Church, of which they themselves rejoiced to be members.

Fourthly, Calvin also objects: "In the Greek Church the unbroken succession of bishops is still preserved, nevertheless, that is not, according to the Roman Church, a true Church, therefore succession is not a Mark of the true Church.

First I respond: The Greek Church cannot show a certain succession; for in the first place, Calvin affirms, in Asia and Egypt, and hence at Antioch, Jerusalem and Alexandria the succession was broken; only the Church of Constantinople remains among the patriarchal seats, which did not appear to lack a proper patriarch. Yet, the Church of Constantinople is not apostolic, nor does it show a certain origin from the apostles, although Nicephorus the patriarch tried to deduce in a Chronology a succession of bishops from Andrew the apostle at Byzantium. Nevertheless, none of the Fathers hand that down, nor was the byzantine Church called apostolic by the Fathers, and the Fathers of the First Council of Constantinople openly affirm that Church in that city is new.[116] Therefore, certainly the Church of Constantinople has some kind of succession from Constantine to the present, but not from the times of the apostles, which is the essence of the question.

I say secondly, the argument we advance from legitimate succession is to particularly prove it is not a Church where there is no succession, which is

---

[115] *Instit.* Bk 4, ch. 2 § 2 and 3.

[116] *Epist. Ad Damasum romanum pontificem.*

42

evident; but it doesn't necessarily follow, that there is a Church where there is a succession. Therefore, by this argument we evidently prove that there is no Church among the Lutherans. On the other hand, that there is no Church among the Greeks, we prove in another way, for without a doubt they were convicted of schism and heresy in three plenary councils, of the Lateran, Lyons and Florence, particularly their heresy denying the procession of the Holy Spirit from the Son, which is a manifest heresy, and Lutherans and Calvinists also affirm that.

Lastly, add that all those patriarchal Churches had manifest heretics for bishops for a long time, and hence the succession of the old shepherds was interrupted.[117]

Fifthly, Calvin objects in the same place that the ancient Fathers, who show the Church from the succession of roman pontiffs, did this because in those times it was certain the faith and religion had not changed in the roman Church; and now the contrary is certain.

I respond: Either Calvin understands that, in those times, the Church was composed of Catholics only, or Catholics together with heretics, because in the Roman Church there was no change in religion. If he assumes the first, he says nothing, for even in this time it is composed of Catholics, but religion has not been changed in the Roman Church. If he asserts the second, he lies. There were not heretics, if all always thought that true faith was in the Roman Church. On that account the Donatists attacked the Roman Church, as now the Lutherans and Calvinists do.

Optatus says: "From where is it, that you contend to usurp the keys of the kingdom for yourselves, O Donatists, who fight against the seat of Peter with your presumptions and bold sacrilege?"[118] St. Augustine adds: "Did you make the seat of the roman Church, in which Peter sat, and in which now Anastasius sits? Why do you call the apostolic seat the chair of pestilence?"[119] And nevertheless, Optatus and Augustine argued from this succession against the Donatists, as we showed above.

---

[117] To couch this in modern terms, Bellarmine is making the distinction between material and formal succession, the former meaning ordaining new bishops, the latter their jurisdiction in the Church. Bellarmine's use of "succession" here refers primarily to formal succession, whereby he says the Greeks have material and not formal succession, and the Protestants have neither. -Translator's note.

[118] Bk 2 *cont. Parmenianum.*

[119] Bk 2 *contra literas Petil.*, ch. 51.

CHAPTER IX
The Sixth Mark

THE SIXTH MARK is the Agreement in Doctrine with the ancient Church. Indeed, the true Church is called apostolic, as Tertullian witnesses, not only on account of the succession of bishops from the apostles, but even on account of the kinship of doctrine, as he says, which is that it retains the doctrine which the apostles handed down. Moreover, it is certain that the ancient Church was the true Church for the first five hundred years, and hence retained apostolic doctrine whereby Theodosius the emperor is praised by Sozomen because by this method he restrained the heretics of his time. He bid the leaders of the sects to come together, thereupon he asked whether they thought the ancient Fathers, who ruled the Church before their separation, which then had arisen from religion, to have thought rightly and truly that the apostles were saints, and when they conceded this, enjoined them: "Then let us examine your doctrine against their writings, and if should agree with them, it may be retained, but if not, let it be thrown out."[120]

Now we can prove in two ways from this Mark that ours is the true Church, and not that of our adversaries. Firstly, by advancing the teachings of the Fathers, whereby we should confirm each of our doctrines. In fact this manner is very lengthy, and more liable to many calumnies and objections. The second way is shorter and more certain, without a doubt by showing first from the confession of our adversaries, that our doctrine is indeed the doctrine of all the ancients. Then showing whether the dogmas of our adversaries were held in the ancient Church by exploring the heresies. Then it will be certain, our doctrine agrees with the doctrine of the ancient catholics, but their doctrine agrees with the doctrine of the ancient heretics.

Thus we proceed to the first. Calvin in his *Institutes* opposed our teaching, and everywhere affirms himself to be against all antiquity. Wherein it follows, that our doctrine is altogether consistent with antiquity. Moreover, he says: "The term 'free will' [*liberum arbitrium*] has always appeared among the Latins,

---

[120] Sozemen, *Hist.*, bk 7, ch. 12.

the term with the Greeks, αὐτεξούσιος, is much more presumptuous."[121] And below that: "I myself should not wish to usurp an expression of this sort, and should others consult me, I would that they abstain from using it."[122] He says the same thing about all the Fathers, with the exception of Augustine, to have brought out human strength, and on free will either to have differed or tottered, that nothing certain could be taken up from their writings.

He so professes that he follows no Father with the exception of Augustine; and a little after, he even deserts Augustine.[123] For he condemns that opinion of Augustine, from his 106th epistle, that our will cooperates with grace, not leading the way, as it were, but following behind, and yet Calvin says it does not cooperate as one who follows behind, but simply everything is done by grace. "And certainly, the opinion of Augustine should not be received in all things, which assigns grace to sanctification, because in the newness of life we are regenerated through the Spirit." Therefore, in the point on grace and free will, Calvin affirms that he is opposed to all antiquity. Likewise, he says: "The error of the Fathers cannot be excused, for they do not attend to the person of the mediator, nearly of the whole doctrine, which is read in the gospel of John, they observe that fasting must be practiced, and intertwine themselves in much speaking."[124] Calvin teaches in this place, that the Son of God was subjected to the Father even with respect to his divinity; and that all the Fathers teach the contrary. He himself says, they all erred, and their error is not excusable.

Likewise, he says: "That which is called 'limbo' is a fable from some subterranean place, although it indeed has great authors, nevertheless it is nothing but a fable."[125] He calls the ancient Fathers the great authors, for he does not usually name the scholastic doctors, unless he uses the term "sophists."

He continues: "Let readers take one thing from Augustine, if they wish to have something on the sense of antiquity. Next, between him and us, this can appear to be the dividing line, what he teaches on the plague of concupiscence, then at length it becomes sin, the will falls with the appetite; but we have that

---

[121] *Instit.*, bk 2, ch. 2 § 4.

[122] *Ibid.*, § 8.

[123] *Ibid.*, ch. 3. § 7.

[124] *Ibid.*, ch. 14. § 3.

[125] *Ibid.*, bk 2, ch. 16., § 9.

itself for sin, which altogether by some cupidity against the law of God, a man is tickled, nay more, depravity itself, which generates lusts of this sort in us, we assert to be sin."[126] Here, he openly declares himself contrary to all the Fathers, and also even to Augustine himself, in the question on concupiscence, which is an extraordinary question. For from this foundation they deduce that true justice is not in us, but merely imputed, and there are no good merits, nay more that all works are sin.

Likewise he adds: "Nearly all the Fathers whose books are extant either fell on this side, where it is treated on satisfaction, or spoke exceedingly roughly and inflexibly."[127] Moreover: "Thirteen hundred years ago it was received in use, that there should be prayers for the dead. But I declare, all the Fathers were snatched into error."[128] He says in the same vein: "I affirm, everywhere the old doctors used the name of merit . . . antiquity sinned . . . antiquity sinned beyond measure in severity, because it required more from a bishop than Paul required and especially celibacy through a succession of time . . . The austerity of the Fathers was beyond measure and can in no way be excused, which both was utterly at variance with the precept of the Lord, and was wondrous in a dangerous way, since they appointed a penance for the sinner in one case seven years, in another for four, and three, and for another for his whole life."[129]

Note, this appears so bitter to Calvin that he himself reckons through faith a man is so justified, that almost nothing remains to be repaid. But if this were true, then he most rightly accuses all the Fathers; hence it follows, that in Calvin's judgment, our teaching on punishment remaining after the remission of the fault was the teaching of all the Fathers.

Nevertheless, Calvin continues to show his break with antiquity: "I do not dare to excuse the Fathers in everything, and they sowed certain seeds of superstition and gave occasion to tyranny, which afterward arose, and then flourished everywhere. The superstitious observation of lent, that every common man thought he must furnish some special obedience to God by those practices, and his pastors commended for holy imitation . . . Therefore, it was

---

[126] *Ibid*, bk 3, ch. 3. § 10.

[127] *Ibid*, bk 3. Ch. 4. § 38.

[128] *Ibid*, bk 3, ch. 15. § 2.

[129] *Ibid*, bk 4, ch. 4 §10; bk 4 ch. 12 § 8.

Calvin really mad when Fathers disagree with Him.

pure κακοζηλία[130] and full of superstition, which ordained fasting under the title and color of the imitation of Christ . . . That marriage was forbidden to the priests, was impious and tyrannical. ”[131] But when it was forbidden, he notes in the margin: Syricius in an epistle to the bishops of Spain. Yet, Syricius sat almost 1200 years ago. And below he adds on this law: "These things which appear to cause reverence in the priesthood, I confess was received with great applause even in antiquity." *Bcm*

Again: "I see many centuries ago, even nearly at the beginning of the Church that the custom was received, that in danger of death the laity should baptize if the minister was not present at that time, I do not see how it can be defended by firm reasoning . . . I do not believe the Fathers can be excused, since they sinned by manner of action; they imitated the Judaic custom of sacrificing more than either Christ ordained or the reasoning of the Gospel would permit."[132] So much for Calvin.

Now the Centuriators of Magdeburg at the end of the chapters *On Individual Centuries*, record nearly all the teachers of those periods taught those dogmas, which we defend today, but that they merely call blemishes of the holy Fathers. And because it would be too long to speak on everything, I will mark only a few things, from the *Centuries*, 2, 3, 4 and 5.

Therefore in the second *Century*, on free will, they say that it was conceded by all the Fathers of this century: "In the same way, Clement asserted everywhere free will, as it appears in the darkness of this sort, not only to have been all the teachers of this century, but even repeatedly to have risen in the following centuries and even to have increased."

It must be noted, that the Lutherans have this point on free will for the foundation of their whole doctrine. Luther says that this point is most rightfully the summation of his affairs, to the extent that the articles on the papacy, on councils and similar things can be called trifles.[133] Therefore, in this particular controversy, and in the very summation of the matter all the Fathers (as the

---

[130] κακοζηλια (kakozēlia) means affectation. Additionally, it is a rhetorical device to make the speaker seem more learned than he is although it is bad form. - Translator's note.

[131] *Ibid*, bk 4, ch. 12 § 20; § 23.

[132] *Ibid*, bk 4, ch. 15, § 20; ch. 18, §21.

[133] Luther, *in assert.* Arctic. 36.

at least they are honest [handwritten note in top-left margin]

Centuriators themselves witness) favor us. Thereupon they say: "The doctrine on justification was more negligently and obscurely handed down by these teachers, and they do not teach that we are justified by faith alone."[134] Moreover, they say: "You shall see in the writings of the teachers of this century, no obscure vestige of the invocation of the saints; . . . All the teachers of this age exalted the martyrs without measure."[135] The Lutherans deny that there is a certain type of baptism of martyrdom, or that sins are expiated in any way through martyrdom.

Continuing, they cite the testimony of nearly all the Fathers of the fourth century, such as Athanasius, Basil, Nazanzien, Epiphanius, Ephrem, Ambrose, and Prudentius on the invocation of the saints, which nevertheless the Centuriators call idolatry.[136]

For the fifth century, they say: "As in the first several ages, the distorted doctrine on free will was invented, so even in this age . . .. Although at times they seem to speak well and correctly, nevertheless, they establish at length that there is free will in matters, even spiritual ones by their overturning of reason . . . Without a doubt this age added good works of men, that which emanates from a contorted doctrine of justification."[137] And immediately they cite much testimony of all the Fathers of that age, even Augustine, that works are meritorious, which they hold as a great error.

Now, against those who say that all the ancients erred, Tertullian elegantly speaks: "All right, now [let us say] every Church would have erred; even the Apostle would have been deceived from his testimony given on certain matters. The Holy Spirit would have regarded no Church, so as to lead it into truth, the purpose for which He was sent by Christ, who asked this from the Father, that he should be the teacher of truth. The overseer, Christ the vicar, would have neglected the service of God, permitting the Church to understand otherwise, believe otherwise than he himself preached through the apostles. And what is like unto it, that so many and so great a number should err in one faith? Therefore, who would dare to say that they might have erred, those who handed down [doctrine]? In whatever manner error came, it reigned of course only as

---

[134] *Centur 2.* Col. 60.

[135] *Centur. 3,* ch. 4, col. 83; col. 85.

[136] *Centur. 4,* col. 295.

[137] *Centur. 5,* col. 500; 506.

long as there was an absence of heresies! The truth waited for some Marcionists and Valentinians to be freed. Meanwhile the Gospel was incorrectly promulgated. To many thousands upon thousands have been imbued wrongly, etc."[138]

Now as we come to the second part it must be set forth, that in the ancient Church those [opinions] which were held as errors were commonly placed in a catalogue of heresies, after being investigated and condemned, by such Fathers as Irenaeus, Jerome, Epiphanius, Philastrus, Augustine, Theodoret, Damascene and by other approved authors: for since these holy and learned men had never dared to simply relate any doctrines in a catalogue of heresies, if they knew there could be some doubt about them in the Church. And on that account we read that there was no one who ever contradicted those Fathers, as it were, whom they did not justly ascribe as a heretic. With this prefaced, we proceed to the catalog.

I. The Simonians taught men were saved according to the grace of Simon, whom they made God, and *not according to just works*, as Irenaeus says.[139] The Eunomians taught in like manner, that sins could not harm any man, if only he had faith, as St. Augustine witnesses. The same Augustine says that this heresy on the sufficiency of faith alone to salvation without works arose in the time of the apostles, from something not properly understood from Paul, and for that reason, the other apostles directed their pen against this heresy in their epistles, that is Peter, John, James and Jude.[140] But this same is the opinion of all the sects of this time.

Luther said: "A man can be pleasing to God in no other way, nor do anything, other than faith; for God cares nothing for works." And again: "A Christian is so rich, that he could not perish even if he wished, no matter how badly he might live, unless he refuses to believe."[141] Albeit Calvin, John of Brenz and certain others tried to some degree to temper this opinion, when they say that good works are necessary; as an effect of faith, nevertheless they still adhere in the same error; for even with that necessity being posited, they teach that works do not merit eternal life in any way, although God requires these as

---

[138] *De praescriptionibus.*

[139] Irenaeus lib. 1., ch. 20.

[140] *De Haeres.*, ch. 54; *De fide et operibus*, ch. 14.

[141] Lib. *De Captivitate Babylonica*, ch. De Eucharistia.

testimonies of faith. This was, however, the very heresy of Simon, who was teaching men to be saved through grace, not through just works. On that account, with that necessity of works being posited, all sects teach that if anyone after committing all crimes should have an act of faith, no sin is imputed to him, which is nothing other than what Eunomius and Luther teach.

II. Thereafter was the heresy of Florinus, that God is the cause of sins, which Irenaeus said is more than a heresy, and even Vincent of Lérin attributed it to Simon Magus in his *Commontorium.* Calvin shamelessly teaches the same thing: "Men sin, not only by the permission, but even by the will of God, so that they pursue nothing by deliberation, unless God would have decreed something among them, and established it by some arcane direction."[142] He also says that Adam fell into sin not only with God's foreknowledge and permission, but even according to his will. A little below that he adds: "Some men scorn to hear the word of God, they are depraved, but into this depravity, they are led by God, that he might show his power and severity among them."[143]

Luther openly taught the same thing: "That wish, in which Judas willed to betray Christ, was a work of God, it was not in the hand of Judas, or of any creature, to change that will."[144] Peter Martyr taught likewise,[145] and Philip Melanchthon in his commentary on Romans, where he says the betrayal of Judas, as well as the conversion of Paul, were the work of God;[146] which commentaries are said to have so pleased Luther, that he said Philip was a second Paul. Nevertheless, Melanchthon retracted the error, both in his work *In Locis* and in his *Apologia* article 19 of the Augsburg Confession.

III. There was a heresy of Origen that the image of God perished in Adam, to which he had been created, as Epiphanius says, who was a witness to this.[147] Calvin teaches the same thing: "Through sin, the heavenly image was

---

[142] *Instit.*, bk 1, ch. 18, § 2.   *denial of FW, God as author of sin.*

[143] *Ibid,* ch. 24, § 14.

[144] *De servo arbitrio.*

[145] *Commentarius,* ch. 2, bk 1 Reg.

[146] *Commentarius ,* ch. 8 ad Romanos.

[147] Epiphanius, *Haeres.*, 64.

obliterated in the first man."[148] Likewise, an error of Origen was that there is no hell, unless it were a horror of conscience, as Jerome tells us in an epistle.[149] Calvin teaches the same thing.[150]

IV. The Peputiani Heretics, as Augustine says, not only gave power to women, but also honored them with the dignity of priesthood.[151] Luther says in those articles, which Pope Leo X condemned, that women can equally absolve in the sacrament of penance, or children, just as a bishop or Pope.[152] And now in this very matter, in England a certain woman is supreme pontiff of the Protestants.[153]

V. The Heretic Proclus said that sin always lives in the reborn; concupiscence is true sin, nor can it be abolished through baptism, but is rendered unconscious as it were by faith;[154] after him, the Messalian Heretics taught the same thing.[155] This is the very opinion of Luther, and likewise Melanchthon and Calvin.[156]

A particular error of the Novatians was that there was not in the Church the power to reconcile men to God, unless through baptism. Afterward they added, that the baptized ought not to be anointed with chrism by the bishop.[157] Such an

---

[148] *Instit.*, Book 2, ch. 2 § 5.

[149] *Ad Avitum.*

[150] *Instit.*, Bk 3, last chapter, § ultimo.

[151] *De Haeres.*, ch. 27.

[152] Article 13.

[153] Here Bellarmine means Queen Elizabeth I, who by the Act of Royal Supremacy of 1534, was the supreme head of the English Church, possessing all the powers which the Pope formerly held and thus, in effect, was a bishop and head of every priest and bishop of the English Church. -Translator's note.

[154] Epiphanius, *Haeres.*, 64.

[155] Theodoret, bk 4, *De hereticis fabulis.*

[156] Luther, *Arctic.* 2 and 31 and in the assertions of the same; Phillipus, *in locis communibus*, ch. De peccato originis; Calvin, *Instit.*, bk 4, ch. 15 § 10.

[157] Theodoret, bk 3, *De haeret. fabul*; Pope St. Cornelius in Eusebius, *hist.*, bk 6, ch. 33.

opinion in the first part is expressly of the Calvinists. For Calvin says there is no sacrament of penance apart from baptism: "But what Jerome said: 'Penance is the second lifeline after the shipwreck,' is obviously impious, and can not be excused."[158] On the other side, it is an error of all the Lutherans. Luther recognized only three sacraments, Baptism, penance and bread. Nevertheless, a little further in the same book, he rejects penance.[159] The Augsburg confession eloquently rejects confirmation, while Calvin says that our Chrism is the oil of the devil and polluted by lies, and on that account the Calvinists anoint their greaves[160] with it, when they can.

VII. Sabellius taught there was one person in God, not three, as Epiphanius witnesses.[161] In our times, Michael Servetus taught the same thing, without any ambiguity, and now this opinion rules in many places.[162]

VIII. St. Jerome says of the Manichees, in his preface of the dialogues against the Pelagians, "It is the mark of these men to condemn nature and remove free will." And St. Augustine adds: "The Manichees do not attribute the origin of sin to free will."[163] All sects openly teach the same thing. Luther says in article 36 that free will is a thing in name only. But in the assertions of the same article, he says it is a name without a substance, and all things happen by absolute necessity. And besides, in the book which he wrote against free will to Erasmus, he placed the title "On the slave will." Calvin did not permit man choice in any matter, so much so that he could not even tolerate the name. Nevertheless, in this, Calvin is more impious than a Manichean, because a Manichean attributed to a wicked god the origin of sin, but Calvin to a good God.

Besides, the Manichees everywhere attacked the Fathers of the old Testament, as Abraham, Sampson, Sarah, Rebecca and the like, as Augustine witnesses. Calvin did the same thing. He says: "Sarah sinned in many ways, when she placed her handmaiden under her husband. But Rebecca, by various

---

[158] Calvin, bk 4, *Inst.*, ch. 19,§ 17.

[159] Luther, *De captivitate babylonica*, ch. De Eucharistia; *ibid,* de extrema unctione.

[160] A Greave is a piece of armor that protects the tibia, or extends from the tibia to the knee. -Translator's note.

[161] Epiphanius, *Haeres.*, 57.

[162] Bk. 1, *de Trinitate.*

[163] *De Haeres.*, ch. 46.

frauds and impostures, corrupted the truth of God, since she procured the blessing of the son by a wicked plan, she deceived her husband, and compelled her son to lie . . . The deed of Judas Machabeus, wherein he offered sacrifice for the dead in Jerusalem, was not without superstition and preposterous zeal."[164] He says that Abraham was an idolater, and "In Sampson, the vicious lust of revenge is in control when he says: 'Fortify me O Lord,' etc." Likewise, Calvin taught that a woman is never allowed to baptize, and adds: "it ought not be dragged out as an example, that Sephora the foolish woman circumcised her son, whereby she gravely sinned in many ways."[165]

IX. The Donatists wanted the Church to consist of the just alone, and also therein deduced that the visible Church had perished in the whole world, but had remained in Africa alone. St. Augustine, who witnessed this, relates that they cruelly cut down Catholics, and especially hated monks and bishops, whom they called Pharisees, and in the first place the Bishop of Rome, whose seat they called the chair of pestilence. Moreover they broke altars, despoiled Churches, sold sacred chalices, gave the Eucharist to dogs, and threw away the sacred chrism.[166]

It is certain that the doctrine and life of the Calvinists is the same, for Calvin teaches that the Church consists of the good alone,[167] as does the Augsburg Confession in article 7. They all teach that the visible Church has perished for many ages, and is now only in northern parts, where they themselves live, particularly Calvin.[168] Next, the Calvinists have left out none of those things which the Donatists blasphemously, or cruelly, or sacrilegiously said or did against Catholics, their sacraments and the altars, etc., but obviously they have done and said many and worse things, which can be seen in the history of Suri and from the book that he recently published, by the title of *De furoribus gallicis*, and from other worthy authors.

X. The Arians taught that the son of God is a lesser being than the Father, as we see in the same citation in Epiphanius. Thereafter, the same Arians did

---

[164] *Instit.*, bk; *Ibid*, ch. 5, § 8.

[165] *Instit.*, bk 3, ch. 14, § 11; ibid ch. 20 § 15; Ibid bk 4 ch. 15 § 22.

[166] *De Unit. Ecclesiae*, ch. 12; bk 2 *contra Petilian*, ch. 51 and 61; bk 3 ch. 40; epist. 163 and elsewhere. Cf Optatus, bk 2 and 6 *contra Parmenian*.

[167] *Instit.*, Bk 4, ch. 1 § 7.

[168] *Instit.*, bk 4, ch. 2 § 2.

not receive any unwritten traditions in any manner, as Maximinus, the Arian bishop taught.[169] Afterwards, many others imitated them, such as Nestorius, Dioscurus and Eutyches, as mentioned in act 1 of the Seventh Ecumenical Council. Therefore, the same Arians committed many and more terrible sacrileges against the sacraments, altars, priests, monks and nuns than the Donatists had, as is clear in the writings of the Fathers of that time.[170]

Many of those who today openly teach the first error of the Arians are called Tritheitae, as can be recognized from the *Prothesibus Valentini gentilis*. And although Luther, Melanchthon, Calvin and others like them hold Arius as a heretic, nevertheless they cannot deny that in their own writings they have sown the seeds of this error, from where these new Arians arose, whom they fight against, as we showed in another work.[171] Moreover, all the heretics of this age teach the second error. The sects of this time reject all traditions, as is clear from their own writings.[172] Next, those cruel and sacrilegious deeds of the Arians, if only the names might be changed, are the ones which the Calvinists everywhere commit.

XI. The Aerian Heretics[173] taught three errors, as witnessed by Epiphanius and Augustine. Augustine noted that he taught: "That it is not fitting to pray or to offer sacrifice for the dead, nor should fasting be established or solemnly celebrated, but rather fasting was to be done when each wished, lest it might appear they were under the law."[174] Thereafter, that no difference ought to be discerned in a priest from a bishop. Epiphanius adds, that they preserved a contrary custom on Friday, even in Lent, and especially ate meat even in Holy Week, and if ever they wished to fast, they usually did so on Sunday and not

---

[169] Quoted by St. Augustine, bk 1, ch. 2 and the last Contra Maximinum.

[170] Athanasius, *Apologia pro fuga sua;* Ruffinus, bk. 11, *hist.*, ch. 3; Theodoret, bk 4, *hist.*, ch. 19 and 20; Victor of Utica, bk 2 and 3 *de Wandalica persecutione.*

[171] In the Praeface to the books *De Christo.* Forthcoming from Mediatrix Press in 2015.

[172] John of Brenz in his prolegomena; Calvin, *Institut.*, bk 4, ch. 8 § 8.

[173] Aerius (not Arius) was a priest of Sebaste in what is now Turkey. -Translator's note.

[174] Augustine, *De haeres.*, ch. 33.

another day.[175]

Nearly all the Calvinists and Lutherans teach and do the same things. Calvin avowedly disputes against praying for the dead. He condemns fasting in Lent and calls it superstitious. Thereupon he says: "The Bishops, priests, pastors and ministers have the same function and duty."[176] The Centuriators of Madgeburg, although they usually number the errors of other heretics, omit those which they recognize to be their own errors. For, when they come to Aerius, because they saw only these three errors were recorded as proper to Aerius, by Epiphanius and Augustine, they could not omit them: Therefore they placed those, but soon added, if there might be nothing else, that these were not errors, but simply contrary positions. Therefore, they affirm these three opinions are common among them which Aerius held to, and they don't deny that in the ancient Church these were held as condemned heresies. From which it follows that the Centuriators, although then not yet born, were heretics of the ancient Church.

XII. Jovinian asserted that man could not sin after baptism, if he had been truly baptized, that is if in reality he had received faith and the grace of God, thereupon abstinence and fasting were not meritorious: on that account, there is equal dignity and merit with virginity and the married life. Wherefore, they even married several nuns with their urging. They also taught all the rewards of the blessed are equal, and what is more, that the Blessed Virgin lost virginity of the flesh by giving birth.[177]

Calvin also holds the first of these errors, since he teaches true faith, which is separated from grace (grace in his understanding), once held, can never be lost, and therefore is nothing except a sign of the elect.[178]

Calvin teaches the second one, when he complains of all of the Fathers because they praised fasting as though it were meritorious.[179]

The third error is of Martin Luther in *Epithalamio*, where commenting on ch. 7 of the first epistle to the Corinthians, he makes four comparisons. The first

---

[175] Epiphanius, *Haeres.*, 75.

[176] *Institut.*, Bk 3. Ch. 5 § 6; *Ibid*, bk 4, ch. 12. § 20; *Ibid*, ch. 3. § 8.

[177] Jerome, bk 1 and 2 *contra Jovinian*; Augustine, bk. *De haeres.*, ch. 82.

[178] *Instit.*, bk 2, ch. 2 § 11 and 12.

[179] *Ibid*, bk 4, ch. 12 § 19. The same error is found in the Augsburg Confession, art. 24, and in citations of Philip Melanchthon, ch. De Mortificatione.

comparison is with chastity as an idea, and there he affirms chastity to be a more noble gift. The second comparison of chastity with matrimony in the presence of God, he says to be equal. The Third comparison is with married women and maidens, and he says: "It behooves us to admit that a married woman excels a maiden in the sight of God." The fourth comparison, is of the state of spouses with the state of religious and ecclesiastics professing celibacy; and he says the state of the married, from its nature, is spiritual, divine, heavenly, and as gold, the state of celibacy is secular, earthly and as a punishment. Similar things are taught by the Augsburg Confession and Calvin.[180]

The Fourth error is of Bucer and Molinaeus. Bucer being the author, affirms in the third part of *Evangelical Union*, that Jesus when he was born, opened the womb of the Blessed Virgin Mary.[181]

The Fifth error is of Luther in a sermon on the birth of the Blessed Virgin Mary, and in the commentary of the first epistle of Peter, where he says that all Christians are holy and just in a measure equal to the Mother of God, from where without a doubt it follows, nearly all are equally blessed.

XIII. Vigilantius also taught many things. First, that the relics of the saints must not be venerated. Secondly, the prayers for the dead from others were not heard, wherein it follows the saints are invoked in vain. Thirdly: that Ecclesiastics ought to be married. Fourthly: it is not expedient to leave behind all things and give to the poor, and, with the world being left behind, to hasten to a state of religion.[182]

Today all the sects teach this. Luther, in his sermon on the Holy Cross, says the relics of the saints are a seduction of the faithful, and therefore they ought to be shut in under the earth; and in his book on the necessity of abrogating the Mass, he affirms that: "God has no greater care of the holy tomb of the Lord than of cattle, for which reason the Apostle says: 'Does God care for cattle?'"[183] He also says that the invocation of the saints is stupid and pernicious.[184] He says

---

[180] Art. 23; Calvin, *Inst.*, bk 4, ch. 13, § 3.

[181] That is, they denied the virginity of Mary *in partu*, (during birth). See St. Peter Canisius, *De Incomparibili Virgini Maria, Dei Genitrix*, book 2. -Translator's note.

[182] Jerome, *Contra Vigilantium*.

[183] *De Abroganda Missa*, parte 3.

[184] *De Eucharistia ad Waldenses*.

the same thing in *Epithalamio:* "Matrimony is a precept of divine law for all, even for ecclesiastics and monks, who do not realize they have the gift of continence." But he calls the gift of continence, not a grace, by which we do not consent to carnal temptations, but one by which we are not tempted, no one has such a gift. Thereupon he dissuades openly from monastic vows and from religion, and only permits that women 60 years old or more, as well as 80 or 100 year old men should remain in monasteries. The Augsburg confession teaches the same thing, for it treats against the articles of the saints, and against the continence of clerics and monks.[185]

Likewise, Calvin treats against the invocation of the saints when he says: "The Papists in their Litanies, Hymns and Sequences, wherein they render something for dead saints, make no mention of Christ,"[186] which is a very crass lie. Calvin continues, however, against the visitation of relics.[187] And in fact the Calvinists burned and cast into the flames the bodies of St. Irenaeus, Martin, Hilary, Bonaventure, etc. Against celibacy of clerics and the profession of monks, Calvin also disputes.[188] Moreover, the Centuriators did not wish to count Vigilantius among the heretics, but they write in that Century, where they say there was contention among two holy priests, that is Vigilantius and Jerome, on relics and invocation of the saints, but treated it as though Jerome debated by shouting, but Vigilantius by solid arguments.[189] In that place they also attribute a certain judgment of Erasmus on the book of Jerome against Vigilantius to Gregory, as if Gregory desired to restrain Jerome. But these issues are taken up in other places.

XIV. The Pelagians taught two things, among others. First, that among men there is no original sin, and especially among the sons of the faithful.[190] Secondly, through whichever sin you like, although it be the lightest, justice

---

[185] Article 21; art. 23.

[186] *Instit.*, bk 3, ch. 20 § 21.

[187] *Ibid.*, bk 4, ch. 13, § 7; *Admonitionem de reliquiis.*

[188] *Ibid.*, bk 4, ch. 12 and 13, whole chapters.

[189] *Centur. 4*, ch. 8, col. 602.

[190] Augustine, *Contra Julianum*, bk 6, ch. 2 and 3; *ad Bonifacium*, bk 4, ch. 2 and 4.

perishes and hence every sin is mortal.[191] The first of these Zwingli eloquently teaches, as well as Bucer and Calvin;[192] except that Zwingli simply denies original sin in any man, and merely teaches that we contracted certain miseries through Adam. On the other hand Bucer and Calvin only deny original sin in the sons of the faithful, whom they say are born saints, and even can be saved without baptism. Every sect teaches the second error.[193] All the rest wish every sin to be mortal by its nature.

XV. The Nestorians taught that in Christ there are two persons and two natures.[194] All the same Fathers condemn this, as Vincent of Lérin witnesses, yet it is the very teaching which Luther, Calvin and all the others furnish remarkably well. The chief error of Nestorius, however, is taught by Theodore Beza, whether from ignorance or from malice, namely in that he places two hypostatic unions in Christ, one of the soul with the flesh, and the other of divinity with humanity.[195]

XVI. In the same time there were also some, I don't know whether they might have been Nestorians also, who taught that the body of Christ does not remain in the Eucharist, if it is preserved on a second day, which St. Cyril calls an insanity.[196] Bucer again devised this error, teaching that in the Eucharist, the body of Christ is not present, except when it is consumed.[197]

XVII. The Monophysites taught that there is one nature in Christ, as one person; so this has been restored in our time. Gaspar Wenckfeld asserts that after the ascension of Christ his human nature was converted into divine, and now is true God, not creature.[198] It appears the same thing, or at some time

---

[191] Jerome, *contra Pelagionaos*, bk 2.

[192] Zwingli, *de baptismo*; Bucerus, *ch. 3 Matthaei*; Calvin, *Inst.*, bk 4 ch. 15, § 20.

[193] Luther, *assert.* Art. 32; Philippus, *in locis*, ch. De discrimine peccati mortais et venialis; Calvin, *Instit.*, bk 2, ch. 8 § 58; bk 3 ch. 4 § 28.

[194] Theodoret, bk 4, *de haeret. Fabulis.*

[195] *De Hypostatica duarum in Christo naturarum unione.*

[196] *Epistola ad Calosirium episcopum.*

[197] See also Conclaeum, tract 8, bk. 3, *Miscellaneorum.* Melanchthon, *in locis*, ch. De coena Domini; Calvin, *Instit.*, bk 4, ch. 17, §39.

[198] *De divina majestate humanitatis Christi.*

something worse, was taught by Brenz, who in a sermon on the Ascension of the Lord teaches: "The humanity of Christ was everywhere, always, by his very incarnation." Jacob Smidelinus teaches the same thing.[199]

XVIII. Xenajas I of Persia openly asserted that the images of Christ must not be venerated, as Nicephorus witnesses.[200] Calvin now asserts the same thing, and he does not wish that the sign of the cross should be raised in any way: wherein he shows himself the brother of the devil, unless he could conquer the devil himself with impiety. For the devil detests the cross because he fears it, and honors it by fear; Calvin detests it, because he despises and also mocks it.[201] He also says that for the first five hundred years there were no images in the temples of the Christians, which is a remarkable lie, since even Calvin himself witnesses the contrary! In the preface to the Institutes, he says that Epiphanius wrote in his epistle to John of Jerusalem, that he saw the image of Christ in the temple, or an image hanging of I don't know which saint. Besides, Lactantius witnesses it in his poem to the crucifix, as does St. Basil in his prayer *in Barlaam*, around the end; Gregory of Nyssa in his oration against Theodore, not far from the beginning, Paulinus on the birth of St. Felicity, Prudentius on S. Cassian, Evodius on miracles of St. Stephen, and St. Athanasius, or whoever is the author of the questions to Antiochus, q. 16, etc. They all teach in their time that images of the saints were in the temples, all of these lived 1100 years ago, as is well known. Add what Nicephorus says, the image of the Blessed Virgin painted by St. Luke, was placed in the temple, which Pulcheria, the sister of Theodosius, set up at Constantinople in honor of the Blessed Virign.

XIX. The Lampetiani taught that monasteries ought to be free, that is, without perpetual vows.[202] In our time Luther teaches the same thing about monastic vows; they cannot be vowed piously in monasteries, unless by this form: "I vow chastity, poverty and obedience even to death freely, that is that I might be able to change my mind, when I wish."[203]

XX. Of certain ones, who denied that the Eucharist is the true body of Christ,

---

[199] *In disputatione Tubingensi,* ch. 34, de Christo.

[200] Bk 16, ch. 27.

[201] *Instit.,* bk 1, ch. 11, § 7; ibid §13.

[202] Damascene, bk. *de centum haeres.,* near the end.

[203] *De votis monasticis.*

and wish it only be a figure or image of the body of Christ; they are related in the VII general Council.[204] Theodoret relates the same thing in a dialogue, long before Ignatius, which is called *Impatibilis*. Zwingli and Calvin teach this heresy in our time.[205]

We have to this point twenty heresies of the heresiarchs, which were condemned by the Church during the first seven hundred years. What we hold as heresies, our adversaries hold as articles of faith; it follows that our doctrine agrees with the doctrine of the ancient Church, but of our adversaries with the ancient heresies.

---

[204] Act 6, tom. 3.

[205] Zwingli, *De verbis coenae Domini*; Calvin, *Instit.*, bk 4, ch. 17 §12.

Union w/ pope

CHAPTER X
The Seventh Mark

THE SEVENTH MARK is the Union of Members among themselves and with the head; for the Church is one body, one spouse, one flock, as scripture teaches everywhere,[206] as well as in the creed of the Council of Constantinople, where we say "one Church." Moreover, the particular union of the body consists in the union of the members with the head, and among themselves. We must speak on each union, even in the first place on the foremost, that of the Roman Pontiff. However, since we have already given a treatise in another place[207] on the Head of the Church, here we merely bring a few testimonies of the Fathers to the fore, whereby we will show that union with the Roman Pontiff was always held as a mark of the true Church among the ancient Fathers.

Irenaeus clearly says, "It is necessary for every Church (that is, those who are, in all respects, faithful) to agree with the Roman Church on account of a mightier pre-eminence."[208] St. Cyprian says: "After those things, still in addition to having constituted for themselves a pseudo-bishop from heretics, they dared to sail to the chair of Peter and the principle Church, from where priestly unity arose, to bring letters from the schismatic and profane, nor did they think they were romans, to whom faithlessness could not have admittance."[209] Speaking on the chair of the Roman Pontiff, he says: "We know we are exhorted, that we should acknowledge the Catholic Church as tree and root and hold fast to

---

[206] Romans XII; Cantic. VI; John X.

[207] See *De Romano Pontifice*, in 5 books by St. Robert Bellarmine, which is found in book one of the De Controversiis. A translation is forthcoming from Mediatrix Press in 2015.
-Translator's note.

[208] Bk. 3, ch. 3

[209] Bk 3, ch. 3.

them."[210] St. Ambrose, in his oration on the death of Satryrus, says: "He asked if he agreed with Catholic bishops, that is, if he agreed with the Roman Church."

St. Jerome, on the noun *hypostasis,* says: "Here, in three parts, the Church is torn, and each is eager to seize me for its own. Meanwhile, I declare: if anyone is joined to the chair of Peter, he is for my part. Meletius, Vitalis, and also Paulinus say they adhere to you. I can believe it if it were asserted by one of them only; as it is, either two are lying or all three."[211] He says also, in an earlier letter (epistle 15): "I unite myself to your beatitude, that is, in communion with the chair of Peter: I know upon that chair the Church was built. Whoever shall eat the lamb outside this house, is profane: if anyone was not in the arc of Noah, he perished while the flood was master. I don't know Vitalem, I spurn Melatius, I have nothing to do with Paulinus. Whoever does not gather with you, scatters, that is, who is not of Christ is of Antichrist." Jerome also adds in an epitaph to Marcellus: "St. Athanasius and his successor, Peter, Alexandrian bishops, dodging the persecutions of the Arian heresy, fled to Rome, as to the safest port of their communion."

Optatus, for some pages from the beginning says, that the first dowry of the true Church is even the especial chair of Peter, which is at Rome, and thereupon it proves that the Donatists do not pertain to the true Church, because they are not joined with Syricius, who was then sitting in the seat of Peter.

St. Augustine, speaking about bishop Cecilianus: "Why wasn't he able to attend to the plotting multitude of enemies, since he saw he was of the Roman Church, in which the preeminence of the apostolic seat always flourished, joined through letters of communication?"[212] He also says: "Come brethren, if you wish, that you might be inserted into the vine. It is painful, when we might see you so cut off: Count the priests, or from the very seat of Peter, in that order of the Fathers who succeeded him: He is the rock, which the gates of hell will not conquer."[213] Pope Leo the Great in his epistle to the bishops of Vienna: "The Lord so wished the oath of preaching the gospel to pertain to the duty of all apostles, that he principally placed it in the most blessed Peter, chief of all the apostles, that his gifts might defuse from that head, as into every head, so that

---

[210] Bk 4, epistol. 8.

[211] *Epistola ad Damasum* on the term "hypostasis" (Epistola 16).

[212] *Epistola 162.*

[213] Psal. Cont. Partem Donati.

I would exhort anyone who had dared to recede from the solidity of Peter, to understand this is itself a divine mystery."[214]

Add to these testimonies experience; we see indeed all those Churches, which divided themselves from that head, just as branches cut away from the root, immediately wither. Certainly the Asiatic and African Church, which so flourished at one time that they had celebrated numerous councils and always held many men, either with respect to doctrine, or sanctity, or very famous, each fortified by God, from that time in which they had made a schism from the Roman Church, they have celebrated no councils, they have had no men with the odor of sanctity, or known for doctrine throughout the whole world, and now they walk in supreme ignorance.

Let us now come to the agreement of the members among themselves. It is certain, concord is a sign of the kingdom of God, which ought to stand in eternity. Discord, however, is of the kingdom of the devil, because, at length, it ought to come to ruin. "Every kingdom divided against itself, will be despoiled."[215] "God is not of dissension, but of peace."[216] And St. Augustine says: "The devil desired to effect through heretics that in the Church of Christ there might be free dissensions, just as there were in the academies of philosophers: that as these through many divisions at length died out, and were consumed by each other, so it will be in the Church."[217]

Now it is very clear from this mark, our Church alone is the true Church of God: Accordingly, in the first place, all the holy writers in our Church wonderfully agreed among themselves, although there were different men in different places, times and languages who wrote, which St. Augustine observes on the matter.[218] Thereupon all decrees of legitimate councils and popes agreed among themselves, even in all dogmas, although they were promulgated by different men, in different places, times, occasions and against very different, nay more, contrary heresies. This is an obvious sign of one and the same Holy Spirit, governing this Church. The diligence of heretics shows this is true, that

---

[214] Leo, epist. 87.

[215] Matt. XII.

[216] 1 Corinth. XIV.

[217] *De Civitate Dei*, bk 18, ch. 32.

[218] *Ibid.*, ch. 41.

although they laboriously pursue all things, nevertheless, they have not discovered anything of any importance which they could condemn; as we showed in the disputation on Councils.

Thereupon, now all Catholics, dispersed throughout the whole world believe the same things on all dogmas of faith. Nor can they think otherwise, since all subject their sense to the sense of one and of the same supreme pastor from the chair of Peter with the counsel of other pastors directing the Church.

There was never any sect of heathen, or of heretics, in which there was such a consensus, and this can easily be shown. First, on the pagan sects, Augustine teaches that both Juno and Hercules, and other gods disagreeing with themselves belonged to the same religion, and even waged war among each other.[219] Concerning all philosophers it was known, as St. Basil says, "It is not fitting that we should fight against the philosophers, since these suffice in their mutual dissensions to overturn the other's doctrine."[220]

The same was the custom of all the heretics, which is most certain. For Irenaeus teaches that the heresy of Simon, the first heresiarch, soon divided, and thereupon were born the sects of Menandrians, Basilidians, Saturinians, etc. In the same place, he writes on the Valentinians, that when they seemed many, there were hardly two, or three who could agree among themselves in every dogma.[221] St. Augustine writes on the heresy of the Donatists that it was cut up into many minute scraps in his time.[222]

The Marcionists were soon divided, and thereupon the Lucianists were born, then the Appellians and Severians, as Epiphanius teaches.[223] The Montinists were divided among Peputians, Artotyritas, Phyrgastas, etc., as Epiphanius writes. The Manicheas also divided into diverse sects, as St. Augustine witnesses. The Messalians, however, were divided into Martyrians, Sathanians

---

[219] *Serm. 11, de verbis Domini.*

[220] Basil, orat. 1, *de opere sex dierum.* Cf. Theodoret, bk. *De Fide;* Augustine, *De Civitate Dei,* bk. 18, ch. 41.

[221] Irenaeus, bk 1, ch. 21; bk 1 ch. 5.

[222] *De Baptismo,* bk 1, ch. 6.

[223] Bk. 1, tom. 3, *contra haereses.*

and Entusiasts.[224] The Arians were soon divided into Acacianos, Macedonians and Eunomians, as can be seen from Ruffinus. The same Arians also changed the faith almost every year, as Hilary writes in each book to Constantine. For equal reason, the Monophysites were so divided that nearly all sects which had existed in the east are children of Eutychus, the author of that heresy, as is certain from Evagrius and Damascene.[225]

In our time, it is certain from a little book on the *Concord of the Students of Luther,* by Fredrick Saphylus. Lutherans were hardly born before they began to be divided into Anabaptists, Confessionists and Sacramentarians; and again, individual sects in some and others even to 34 different ones, and this was in the time of Staphylus. Now, however, they number nearly 100 very different sects advancing one Luther. Yet this happened by the providence of God; for in this way heresies consume themselves; indeed their division is not mathematic, which proceeds into infinity. Wherefore the Prophet Isaiah says: "I will make the Egyptians to attack the Egyptians."[226] And St. Hilary adds: "War for the heretics is peace for the Church."[227]

Add to that, even the same heretical authors do not agree with themselves, which is most certainly a mark of a false doctrine, as Luther himself says: "Lies, you cannot more certainly show except when they are contrary to themselves. It has indeed been ordained by God, that the impious shall always confound themselves, because lies do not agree, but always witness against themselves."[228] Next, John Cochlaeus collects the innumerable contradictions of Luther in *Septicipite,* where he throws out at the end, 36 different opinions of the same Luther on one article, that is, on communion under both kinds. The Augsburg Confession also, which they all hold to be sacred, they so changed and edited differently, that they themselves do not know which might be the true Augsburg Confession, on which matter you can consult Harmoniam of Andrew Fabritio Leodi, where you will see apart from the remaining edition of 30 years,

---

[224] Epiphanius, bk. 1, tom. 3, *contra haereses*; bk. 2 tom. 1; *haeres.*, 80.; Augustine, *de haeres.,* ch. 46.; Theodoret, bk. 4, *de haeretic. Fabul.*; Ruffinus, bk. 10, *hist.,* ch. 25.

[225] Evagrius, bk. 3 and 4, *histor.*; Damascene, bk. *de centum haeresibus.*

[226] Isaiah XIX.

[227] *De Trinitate,* bk 7.

[228] *De Votis Monasticis.*

there is even an edition of 40 years which is double the size of the other.

Yet our adversaries respond to this argument as they can. Firstly, Calvin, in the preface of the *Institutes*, says that it is no wonder if from their religion soon divisions should rise, as well as contrary sects, for it also happened to the Church of the apostles; indeed, Simon came from these, and Nicolaitae, etc. The Devil is truly always present where he sees good seed is sown and he comes and sows over it cockle. Thereupon, the same Calvin says, from this mark can be gathered, that the Catholic Church is not the true Church since there are as many assemblies of schismatics and divisions as there are monasteries. Formerly, indeed monks lived separated from others, but they did not partake of the sacraments separately; nay more they ran to the Churches of the ordinary ministers, and there with the rest of the people entered into sacred things. But now, each monastery has erected a private altar for itself, and they partake of the sacraments separate from the Christian people, which they witness by their names, since some are called Benedictines, other Franciscans, still others Dominicans. Thirdly, some add more sects, Thomists, Scotists and the like, which are among us.[229]

I respond to the first: This is the distinction between the division of heretics from the Church, and the division from some heresy, because in the Catholic Church, a certain rule is discovered of settling controversies, that is the opinion of the supreme pastor, or of a general council, and therefore dissension does not arise from the doctrine of the Church, but from the malice of the devil alone. On that account, in every respect wherein they arise, they are soon condemned, and after the heretic has been thrown out, the fissure is restored, it makes no more progress in the Church herself. But with the heretics, there is not any rule of ending the controversy. Indeed, each wants to be put in charge of others and to be the judge of others, and thereupon it happens, as that ordinarily each new heresy you like soon after gives birth to others, and others, until through many divisions it is consumed, so that it would seem a miracle if some heresy should endure for a long time. Therefore the doctrine of the Church in itself gives birth to union and association of souls: but heresy in itself, and from its own nature, blossoms forth into divisions and schisms. Since we shall look at the manner of other heresies, the Lutheran sect was soon divided into so many other sects, and daily more and more it is divided, nor is it hoped by them that there will be any end to the division, we rightly judge them heretics, and at length, the name of Lutheran will utterly perish.

---

[229] *Instit.*, bk 4, ch. 13., § 14.

I speak to the second argument: in the first place, it is a lie of Calvin that the ancient monks did not have their own altar, but received the sacraments in the Churches of ordinary parishes. For Epiphanius, in his letter to John of Jerusalem witnesses that they ordained Paulinianus a priest in the monastery of St. Jerome, who confected the sacraments in that very monastery with the rest of the monks, because St. Jerome, because of humility, did not dare to offer the sacrifice of the altar too often. Likewise, Cassian tells that in the desert itself, monks had their own priests, there were even monks who ministered the sacraments to the others.[230] St. Augustine teaches that not only in solitude, but even in cities, such as Milan and Rome, monks had put a priest in charge of their monasteries; without a doubt it was a priest, since was to confect the sacraments in the monastery, so that the monks would not be compelled to go out from the monasteries in order to go to the Churches.[231] Thereafter, St. John Damascene wrote in his history on Barlaam and Josaphat, that Barlaam celebrated the sacrifice of the Mass in his cell, while Josephat alone was present as his minister.

I say in the second place, a schismatic can not materially become anything else on account of a different altar, rather formally; otherwise all parish priests would be schismatics, because they have different altars in the same city. And all bishops would be schismatics, because they have different altars in different cities. Therefore, they alone are schismatics, who erect a proper altar, so as to esteem the altar of others as profane. Thereupon it is evident that the monks of this time are not schismatics by this very fact, because they obey the one supreme pontiff, are ordained priests by ordinary bishops, and thus are frequented by the people. Next, the names of the orders, Benedictine, Franciscan, Dominican, etc., are not taken up from the author of some doctrine, but from the one who established a more severe discipline, as has been noted.

I say to the third objection, Thomists and Scotists do not disagree, unless it is in those matters which do not pertain to faith, as St. Augustine says on the dissensions of teachers in his time;[232] and on that account they and every Catholic always subject themselves to the Church's definition. Hence, although they seem to oppose each other with words, nevertheless in the business itself they all agree in matters of faith; since all profess themselves to believe that one doctrine, which has been judged to be something which must be believed in the

---

[230] Cassianus, *collat. 18*, which is of the abbot of Pyamon, ch. 15.

[231] *De moribus Ecclesiae*, bk 1, ch. 31.

[232] *Contra Julianum*, bk. 1.

Roman Catholic Church.

But heretics disagree on particular matters of faith, and one holds the other as a heretic, and nevertheless they recognize the same Luther as a father.[233] Moreover, our adversaries cannot deny it by any reasoning: Accordingly, the Anabaptists would not deny that they are heretics to the Lutherans and Zwinglians, and the other way around; and nevertheless they all proceeded from the same Luther. The Zwinglians are heretics to the remaining Lutherans, as is certain from the testament of Brenz, and in many books of Luther. Zwinglians and Calvinists, however, do not dare to detest Luther, but in very serious matters they disagree with him, as is clear from the books of Calvin, Beza, and Peter Martyr, on the Lord's super, and on the place of Christ's body.

Again among the Confessionist Lutherans, rigid and lax seriously contend with each other. It appears so from the books of Johan Wigand and Illyricus against George the elder and Philip Melanchthon, and of the latter against the former. The Centuriators in the preface to the 5th century speak thus about themselves: "Although some are still teachers of the Church of God dispersed in different places, nevertheless they are not only by the children of this age, but even by their own fellow laborers and confreres, mocked, molested, afflicted, beaten down and broken, while they proclaim them stoic and seditious: even as the crimes of sedition and heresy dash against them."

John Wigand says in his book on the error of George the elder: "You, O George, are that man, who disturbs Israel, not we, who warn you on the foul errors opposed to the word of God. For you have brought forth cockle and foul errors into the Church of God with books, and disseminated them far and wide, and propagated them. But we exhort the Church of God, as in truth, and once recognized and accepted with purity of doctrine by God for salvation the organ of Luther shall stand firm." And below, after a fourth error: "George glories in great boldness, lest he would cut one hair from the doctrine of Luther, and meanwhile the whole doctrine of Luther on free will, he attributes to a base mind and the devil in the chair of Luther." Even further, after a seventh error, he says: "The man of God, Luther, destroyed and publicly refuted those pernicious errors of [George] the Elder both in his writings and disputations."[234]

In addition, a very serious question amongst the rigid arose on original sin. For Illyricus contends the sin of origin was a substance, and he calls the contrary

---

[233] Cf., Cardinal Hosius, *contra Brentium*, bk. 1; St. Peter Canisius, in his preface to the books of Vega printed at Cologne.

[234] Wigand, *De errore Georgii Majoris.*

opinion a Pelagian specter. Conversely, Johan Wigand, Tilman Hesch, and others write against Illyricus, as if he were a manifest Manichean. Certainly Hesch, from the beginning of the *Remedy Against Illyricus*, teaches that this question pertains to the foundations of faith.

Thereupon, from the same province of Saxony, within ten years contradictory opinions went out, published under public names, on the most serious matter of all. For in the synod of Dresden, around 1571, while celebrating common consensus they rejected the teaching of Brenz, Illyricus and others on the person of Christ, and nevertheless, that very opinion was condemned by them in 1580 in the *Book of Concord*, which they had publicly received; and as the synod and the Concord of Wittenberg were published, they bore before themselves the authority of the same prince.

CHAPTER XI
The Eighth Mark.

THE EIGHTH MARK is Holiness of Doctrine. Indeed, the true Church is not only Catholic, Apostolic and one, but also Holy, as the creed of the first council of Constantinople holds. It is certain that the Church is called "holy," because her profession is holy, containing nothing false with respect to doctrine, and nothing unjust with respect to a doctrine of morals. Wherefore, in Psalm 18, the law of the Lord is called immaculate, faithful testimony, a clear precept of the Lord. Evidently from this mark is shown no Church is true but ours. Indeed, there is no sect of the Pagans, or of the Philosophers, or of the Jews or Turks, or Heretics, which will not contain some errors, tried and manifestly contrary to right reason.

Concerning the pagans, it shows the worship of many gods is absurd and foul, as many of the Fathers understood,[235] and there is not anyone that doubt this matter today.

On the ancient philosophers Theodoret teaches the same thing in his book on the Laws, which is the ninth to the Greeks, where he teaches Lycurgus permitted adultery to be legal: in the laws of the Persians, incestuous marriages were permitted between mothers, sons and sisters. In the laws of the Massagetae, those who were going to die or were old could be eaten by their neighbors. In the laws of Tibareni, the old were thrown from high towers, in the laws of the Armenians, dead bodies of men were thrown to dogs: in the laws of the Scythians, the living who had offended them were buried with the dead. In the Laws of Plato, which appeared to be the best of all, the most outrageous vices were prescribed or praised, as the sharing of wives, wicked lust, abortion, infanticide and like things.

As to the Muslims, the same is clear from the Qur'an. For it teaches that all are saved by their laws, if they should keep them, be they Jews, Christians or Turks.[236] It also teaches everywhere that the beatitude of the future life consists in food and drink, and a multitude of wives, while no mention is ever made in the whole Qur'an of the vision of spiritual actions, or the love of God. In chapter 43 it says that God and the angels pray for Muhammad. Similar very absurd

---

[235] Minucius Felix, in Octavio; Arnobius, bk 4, 5, 6, and 7 contra gentes; Augustine, de Civitate Dei, bk 7.

[236] Ch. 2, c. 5, 28, 47, 48.

things are everywhere read in the Qur'an.

From the Jews that wrote after the coming of Christ, it is manifest from their books. For in the first place, in the doctrine of the Talmud, which is their written word, not God's, innumerable errors are discovered.[237] Rabbi Solomon, whom the Jews reckon to be the greatest, teaches in his commentary on Genesis on that verse: "This now is bone from my bones," that Adam had sexual intercourse with all the beasts and wild animals, and he could not satisfy his lust until he at last embraced Eve.[238] The same rabbi, in his commentary on Numbers, in that verse *On the first day offering holocausts to the Lord*, he selects "the holocaust of the Lord," and says it is a precept to offer a holocaust on the day of a new moon for the sin of God, which he committed when he diminished the light of the moon.[239] The same Rabbi Solomon tells such a fable in chapter 1 of Genesis, on that verse "Two great lights;" and the same in chapter 4 of Deuteronomy, in that: God created man," he says Adam was so grown, that he could touch heaven with his head, while he was on earth. Similar things occur everywhere in the books of the Jews.

Concerning the ancient Heretics the same thing can be shown. Indeed, there was almost no heresy which did not have manifest errors. The Gnostics taught, among other things, that they ought to practice orgies, and that every lust should be exercised, nevertheless they shunned conception. If by chance conception should follow, they would extract from the womb of the pregnant woman, and grind it in a mortar, and devour it as a condiment like honey and pepper; and in this way they said they celebrated the great Pasch.[240]

The Carpocratiani taught that everyone was held to perpetrate every kind of wickedness, and if or when they died, they had not perpetrated everything, they said their souls would be sent back to their bodies, and this as often as it took to fill the measure of crimes, and in this way they explained that part of the

---

[237] See Sixtus Senensem, bk 2, *Bibliothecae Sanctae.*

[238] *Comment. Cap. 2 Gen. In illud Hoc nunc os ex ossibus meis; dicit Adamum cum omnibus bestiis, et feris carnaliter congressum, nec potuisse libidinem explere quousque ad Evae amplexus pervenit.* This is Bellarmine's summary of that line in the Talmud. -Translator's note.

[239] In ch. 28, *Numeri.*

[240] Epiphanius, *de Haeresi,* 26.

Gospel: "You will not go from there, until you will have paid the last farthing."[241]

The Montanists made sacrifice from the blood of year old infants, whom they wounded with small copper pins, the whole of which they squeezed out with incredible cruelty.[242]

The Manicheans taught it was just as much a sin to pluck a leaf from a tree and murder a man. The same asserted parts of the divine essence were held captive by the princes of darkness, and from them some are liberated, the others are condemned for eternity.[243]

The Donatists made martyrs for themselves, by casting themselves headlong off a mountain, or suffocating themselves or throwing themselves into the fire, or threatening death and killing those who refused to kill themselves.[244] Infinite things of this kind can be added.

The sects of our time teach that every man is justified by means of individual faith alone, whereby each believes for certain that he is just in the sight of God on account of Christ, which can be compared with any paradox you like. For it is plainly not above reason, or apart from reason, but entirely contrary to it. I ask, therefore, were I to begin to believe that I am justified, whether I am or not; if I am justified, therefore, I am not justified through the faith by which I believe I am justified, because that faith comes after my justice; if I am not justified, therefore, that faith is false and it is not divine justifying faith, unless we might say, men are justified through a lie.

Besides, every Lutheran particularly extolls the spirit of prayers and invocation, and yet this faith abolishes the Lord's prayer. For if I believe for certain, that I have no sin, I would be a liar were I to say with this faith: "Forgive us our trespasses." On that account, Calvinists altogether condemn the Anabaptists, for they do not think they are justified, or saved, unless they turn from their errors, and nevertheless they know the Anabaptists believe for certain that they are just, therefore they are compelled to say they are just and not just at the same time.

Besides this common dogma, each holds their own doctrines, full of manifest absurdity. The Anabaptists, more than any other, have many night assemblies

---

[241] *Ibid.*, 26.

[242] Augustine, *De Haeres.*, 26.

[243] *Ibid.*, 46.

[244] Augustine, *Epist. 50*; Theodoret, *De Haeret. Fabulis.*, bk. 4.

wherein they marry dogs, as is collected from their articles, which John Cochlaeus refuted, and they even took their own sisters openly as wives. Article 11 of the Anabaptists is: "No man ought to publicly preach;" and article 17: "prayer should be done after the sermon, in order that they might be fruitful and multiply." Article 19: "it is permitted for a brother to take his true sister as a wife."

The Lutherans hold that very manifest error as their own, namely, that infants, while baptized, use reason, so that they hear the word of God, believe, and love, which is in the Wittenberg synod of 1536. Nevertheless, that is opposed to truth, as St. Augustine writes, those who say this do injury to the human senses. How credible is it that an infant who weeps and struggles as much as it can while it is washed, understands what is going on? Next, the Calvinists have as their own teaching that is not only opposed to piety, but also to reason, that everything which happens does so by absolute necessity, even so much that God is the cause of all sin, wherein nearly all Lutherans disagree with them.

But our Church, the Catholic Church, teaches no error, no foul thing, nothing contrary to reason, although many things are above reason. Hence, it alone is absolutely holy, and to her alone corresponds what we say in the Creed: *I believe in the holy Church*. This matter the Fathers showed against not only the pagans,[245] but also the heretics, as St. Thomas most accurately shows in the *Summa Contra Gentiles*.

Therefore, we conclude with St. Augustine: "Nothing filthy and wicked is set forth to be gazed at or imitated in christian Churches; but either precepts of the true God are recommended, his miracles narrated, his gifts praised, or his benefits implored... Truth was seen to be not contradictory to reason, but only different from custom."[246]

---

[245] Justin Martyr in both apologies; Tertulian, *Apologeticus*, ch. 36,sqq.; Arnobius, bk. 1, 2, and 3, *contra Gentes*; Minutius Felix, *Octavius*; Augustine, *de Civitate Dei contra Paganos*.

[246] *De Civitate Dei*, bk. 2, ch. 28; bk. 22, ch. 7.

CHAPTER XII
The Ninth Mark

THE NINTH MARK is the Efficacy of Doctrine. Only the true Church has doctrine that is not only immaculate, but even converts souls, as is said in Palm 18, a living sermon penetrating even to the division of the soul and spirit (Hebrews 4). Although the ancient philosophers displayed great wisdom, and persuaded people of their laws with supreme eloquence, nevertheless they never could even draw a nearby town to their laws, as Athanasius and Theodoret teach.[247] Because their words were not living words, but dead, not of the spirit of God, but of the spirit of men. On the other hand, the Muslims dragged many but by the terror of arms, not by force and efficacy of doctrine, for indeed Muhammad himself teaches in the Qur'an that men must be compelled to the faith by war.[248] Next, the heretics are never read to have converted any heathens or Jews to the faith, but only to have perverted Christians, which even Tertulian recorded: "Why should I speak on the cheat of their ministry? Since it is their business not to convert the heathen, but overturn us, they undermine our [side], and build up their own."[249]

But you might say with Freculph in his Chronicle,[250] that in the time of the emperor Valens the whole race of the Goths was converted from paganism to Arianism.

I respond: The Goths, were not converted by the Arians, but wretchedly deceived. Indeed, the Goths who already for a long time had gone out from their borders and fought under the auspices of the Roman Empire, and heard many excellent things about Christians, from their own will, with no one impelling them, asked for bishops from the emperor, by whom they should be taught, and it is said they were prepared to believe anything from them. But the Emperor, since he was an Arian, sent Arian bishops, and thus the Goths were miserably deceived, since they wished to be made Christians, but were made Arians,

---

[247] Bk *de Humanitate veri*; Thedoret *de legibus*.

[248] Chapter 18 and 19.

[249] *De Praescript. Haeret.*

[250] Bk. 4, ch. 20.

nevertheless not by any virtue or miracles of the Arians. For, how difficult is it to pour poison drop by drop into a man who is prepared to receive it? Moreover, Freculph does not relate this history in full: it is certain from Socrates, Sozomen and Theodoret,[251] that the greater part of the Goths were Christian and Catholic, but were afterward deceived by Arians. Therefore, heretics do not convert men to the faith, nor can they. For heretics indeed have the Scripture, but they do not have the true sense of the Scriptures, which properly is the sword of the spirit. Indeed the words are not a sword, but a scabbard, wherein the sword of the spirit is contained. Therefore, since these do not fight with a sword, but only with a scabbard, it is little wonder, if they do not strike the hearts of infidels? Neither should it be a wonder that they pervert Catholics, for men are prone to going down to the wide and easy road, which these open up for them. And God permits this to happen on account of the ingratitude of those who were once enlightened, and who did not respond to the light they had received with good works.

Whereas, truly the holy and apostolic Church once, in a short time and through contemptible men, drew the whole world by means of an external splendor, without arms and pomps. The whole world, that is great men as well as the small, the learned and unlearned, young, old, men and women. And it drew them not to the delights of this world, but to things which must be believed beyond all reason, and to the cross, the narrow and most perfect way, which is repugnant to flesh and blood, and all these things on account of no reward in this life, but only in the future life. And it so persuaded this, that many preferred more to lose all riches, honors, friends, relations and even their own life, than the faith of Christ.[252]

Thereupon, from the time of St. Gregory even to our times, even from the testimony of our adversaries, many can be proved to be converted by the Catholic Church. For, in the Sixth Century, at the bidding of St. Gregory, not the heretics (who even then were not lacking), but monks and bishops converted the pagan English to the faith of Christ, as the Centuriators of Magdeburg attest.[253]

---

[251] Socrates, bk. 4, ch. 27; Sozomen, bk. 6 ch. 37; Theodoret, bk. 4, last chapter.

[252] Athanasius and Theodoret, loc. Cit.; Augustine, *de Civitate Dei*, ch. 5, where he places among the greatest miracles, that a few apostles by means of only the efficacy of the divine Word, conquered the whole world without eloquence or arms.

[253] Centuriators, *Cent. 6*, ch. 2, col. 37.

Thereafter, in the time of Pope Conon, St. Kilian was sent by the Pope to convert the Franks, as the Centuriators themselves say.[254]

After that, in the times of Gregory II and Gregory III, and Zachary, a great part of Germany was converted to the faith, not by the Iconoclast heretics, who then abounded in the world, but through St. Boniface, a bishop and martyr, whom Pope Gregory II had sent, as the Centuriators affirm: "In this century, after the time had dawned, which the Lord in his mercy had determined, the matter succeeded with greater fruit. For the Lord raised Vinofridus, whom the Romans call Boniface, who, with his colleagues, propagated their Churches in Germany, and he governed and advanced the work of their hands."[255]

In the preface of the same Century, they blasphemously and with the greatest ingratitude speak thus about St. Boniface, their own apostle: "The pope had at hand his hand picked galley slaves, very skilled in this sort of bird-catching, bold and rash, who enticed and entangled in rewards and honors, did their best with zeal in all nations and kingdoms . . . Such a galley slave was Boniface, called the apostle of the Germans, who so brooded over this supreme study of skill and force that all Germany was reduced to the power of the roman pope. Although in several places it is told that he abolished pagan idolatry, nevertheless he did not sow the seed of pure and incorrupt christian religion . . . That pseudoapostle, inflated with such insolence that not only did he despise all counsels from on high, but he even maliciously brought in that roman tyranny just as heretics and disturbers of the Church." Here, the Centuriators seem to have forgotten that St. Boniface was a papist since they speak so well of him! Behold how they treat the apostle of Germany, whom every historian of that time speaks about with the greatest honor.

Thereafter, the Centuriators affirm that the monks of Morbejen converted the Vandals, and that the Bulgarians, Slavs, Poles, Danes and Moravians were converted in that century, but subjected to the Roman Pontiffs, wherein they prove these nations were converted by Papists. Likewise, they record that many kings and peoples were converted by the work of the Emperor Henry I, Bohemia by Adalbert, and Moravia by Methodius, whom nobody can deny to have been Papists, since it is certain that they were subject to the Roman Pontiffs.[256]

The Centuriators continue on, and teach that in the 11th century a great part

---

[254] *Cent. 7*, ch. 2, col. 31.

[255] *Cent. 8*, ch. 2, col. 20.

[256] *Cent. 9*. Ch. 2, col. 15; Cent. 10, ch. 2, col. 18 and 19.

of the Hungarians were converted, and were given bishops and confirmed by the Roman Pontiff, this confirmation at the request of King St. Stephen of Hungary who had recently converted.[257]

After those times, similar conversions were not lacking in the Catholic Church. Accordingly Pope Adrian IV, before his pontificate, was sent by Pope Eugene to convert Norway to the faith, as Platina and others attest; and unless I am mistaken, the Centuriators themselves attest to this in their 12th or 13th edition, at least I hear, I have not seen it yet. It is also certain in this century that St. Vincent, a Dominican, converted twenty thousand to the faith, both Jews and also Saracens, as St. Antoninus, who was a contemporary, writes.[258]

Lastly, in our own time many thousands of nations have converted to the Catholic faith. Some of the Jews also in individual years were converted and baptized at Rome by Catholics devoted to the Roman Pontiff, and even the Turks have not been lacking, who were converted both at Rome and at other places. On the other hand, the Lutherans have scarcely converted one or the other, although they compare themselves with the apostles and the evangelists, and they have many Jews in Germany, and in Poland, and in Hungary there are many Turks nearby. St. Augustine then, most properly, compares heretics with partridges, who gather the young which they have not produced, while on the contrary the Church is like a most fertile dove, which daily brings forth new young.

---

[257] Centur. 11, ch. 2, col. 27.

[258] 3 pars hist. Tit. 23, ch. 8 § 4.

Chapter XIII
The Tenth Mark

THE TENTH Mark is the Holiness of the Authors, that is, of the first Fathers of our religion. Indeed, the true Church does not only have holy and efficacious doctrine, but even holy teachers, and famous with respect to the glory of their deeds. Now we will speak on uprightness, and afterward on miracles.

Now if one were to consider the great teachers of the Catholic Church, first the patriarchs and prophets, thereafter the apostles, then the doctors, who struck against individual heresies, and at length the establishers of the religious orders, he will discover they were all so holy, chaste, pious and sober, that our adversaries shall have nothing which they might condemn them for, except an excess of holiness. St. Augustine says the same things about the monks of his time, and on Catholic teachers: "These are learned bishops and shepherds, deep in holiness, keen defenders of truth, who took in the Catholic faith in their milk and ate it in their food, of which milk and bread they administered to small and great alike. With such, after the apostles, the Holy Church increased by means of such planters, irrigators, builders, shepherds and nourishers."[259] Add to this, that Luther himself affirmed Bernard, Dominic and Francis to have been saints, as well as Philip Melanchthon and others from our adversaries.[260]

But the teachers of the heathen were either light poets, or proud philosophers, and impure on each side. For the particular wise men of the Greeks were impure beyond measure, to such an extent, that they were even infamous among their own rites, particularly on account of their vices against nature, as Athenaeus witnesses,[261] and on our side Theodoret in his book on the Laws, and clearly even St. Paul himself.[262] Muhammad however, could contrive nothing more incontinently, for he himself in the Qur'an, says that he has received the privilege from God to marry every woman which he might have

---

[259] *De moribus Ecclesiae*, ch. 31; *in Julianum*, bk. 2.

[260] Luther, *De Captivitate Babylonica*, ch. 2; Melanchthon, *Apolog.*, Art. 5, and 27.

[261] Bk. 13, ch. 27.

[262] Romans I: 25.

loved, even if they were kin.[263]

On the heresiarchs many things can be said, but one is the common vice of all; pride. St. Augustine says: "In different places, there are different heresies, but pride, as one proud mother, begot them all, just as our one Catholic mother has begotten all faithful christians diffused throughout the whole world."[264] Certainly no heresy is discovered from intention, devised in itself, but *per accidens* from some wicked occasion, as monsters are usually generated.

Egesippus, as quoted by Eusebius, says this on Theobute, the first of all heretics: "Then, the Church was called maiden, because she had not yet been corrupted by the deceit of an adulterous word, but then a certain Theobutes, because he merited the rebuff of the episcopacy, began from the beginning to disturb and corrupt all things.[265]

After this rose Simon Magus, who, it is certain from Acts chapter 8, had canvassed for episcopal authority, and wished to give money so as to buy it. After he was excluded, he devised a new heresy, that one who could not be in the Church, at least could rule it on the outside.

A little after Simon Magus, Valentinus came, about whom we learn from Tertulian. In his book, *contra Valentinianos*, he said: "Valentinus had hoped for an episcopate, since he was possessed of genius and eloquence, but being unworthy, another was put in charge of the place from the prior right of testimony, he broke from the Church of the authentic rule (as those with a mind for rule usually do, excited with the presumption of enkindling revenge), etc.

Thereafter arose Marcion, of whose beginning St. Epiphanius tells us: "Marcion was raised up by ambition, after he did not receive the presidency he went into the Church, and devised counsel for himself. . . with emulation therefore, he was both moved to great indignation and filled with pride he planned to make a divide, raising a heresy after himself and saying: 'I will cleave your church and I shall leave it broken forever.' Really, he did cause no small division, but he did not break the Church, which is truth itself no those who obey her."[266]

On Montanus, Theodoret writes: "He, by ambition, was moved with the lust

---

[263] *Qur'an*, ch. 43.

[264] *De pastoribus*, ch. 8.

[265] Eusebius, *hist.*, bk. 4, ch. 22.

[266] *De Haeres.*, 42.

of obtaining the first place, and called himself the Paraclete."[267] On Novation he writes the same thing according to Cornelius in his epistle: "He relates that with lust of the episcopacy, which he conceived secretly within himself, he fell into ruin in all these matters."[268] Epiphanius says on Sabellius: "He was brought to greater arrogance and madness, he said he was Moses, and his brother Aaron."[269] Theodoret says that Arius, "Since he was related to a great number of the priests of the Alexandrian Church, and he saw a great Alexander sitting in the pontifical seat, was struck with envy; and when he pursued the matter battles against him commenced, thus he discovered the occasion for impious dogmas."[270]

Epiphanius speaks on the heresy of the Semi-Arians: "Therefore, they came to contention, again the same with their companions, on account of a certain hatred and human rivalry, quarrels broke out among themselves, arguing about the primacy."[271] The same author adds on Aerius: "When Eustachius came to the episcopacy, Aerius desired it more, but did not attain it. Hence arose their rivalry."[272]

Theodoret writes that: "Nestorius spent a great part of his life capturing the favor of the people with a swarthy vestment, faking paleness, composed with words, until at length he attained to the episcopacy." Likewise, Socrates writes on the heresiarch Sabbatius: "Moreover he burned with the desire of attaining the papacy."[273] John Wycliff, because he could not be a bishop, became a heresiarch, as Thomas Walden writes.[274]

In the same way, our adversaries certainly cannot deny that the sects of this time rose from ambition, pride, envy and hatred. For first, the beginning of all

---

[267] Bk. 3, *de haereticis fabulis.*

[268] *In epist. Ad Fabium*, bk. 6; *hist.*, ch. 35.

[269] *Haeres.*, 57.

[270] Theodoret, *de hereticis fabulis*, in the beginning, bk 4.

[271] Epiphanius, *haeres.*, 73.

[272] *Ibid.*, 75.

[273] Socrates, *Hist.* Bk. 5, ch. 20.

[274] Bk 2, *Doct. Fid.*, ch. 60.

the heresies of this time was certainly the envy and ambition of Luther, as he was angry when the office of promulgating indulgences was transferred from his order of monks to the Dominicans, as John Cochlaeus writes in the acts of Luther in the year 1517. Wherefore (as the same relates a little after in the acts of the year 1519), in the first disputation that was held in Lisius between Luther and Eck, Luther exclaimed: "This case neither began on account of God, nor will it be ended on account of God." He says the same thing in his epistle to Argentienses, that he would gladly deny the body of Christ to be in the Eucharist, if the Scriptures were not so clear, because by this reasoning it seemed that he could be more of a hindrance to the papacy.

Luther boasts such pride in his book against the king of England,[275] that he said kings, princes and popes were not worthy to answer his correction of their blindness. He willed that he be held as a holy man, whether men wished or no, and made his teaching greater than that of a thousand Cyprians and a thousand Augustines. And in the book *De Missa Angulari*, so as to prove that he has for his own Father, he who is the king of all the sons of pride, as he says he was taught by the devil, that the Mass might be a wicked thing, and convinced by the reasoning of the devil to abolish the Mass. Thus, such was the wickedness of Luther, that even his own could not tolerate him. For Conrad Genserus writes on this, that in all his collections of books: "That point must not be concealed, that Luther was an impatient man of a forceful genius, even that he should be unwilling to consider anything unless it agreed in all things with himself." And further on: "The Lord saw to it, lest he should be a nuisance to his Church by contention and effrontery of the mouth, whose rattling he formerly so happily advanced."

The Protestant Ministers of Zurich, in response to a book which Luther had written against Zwingli, say: "Prophets and Apostles are zealous for the glory of God, not private honor, nor pertinaciousness and pride. Yet Luther seeks his own, he is pertinacious, he conducts himself with excessive insolence, and in all his corruptions he is for the most part discovered to be of a malignant spirit, which scarcely is found in a friend or a paternal mind." All the disciples of Luther are the same, and if from their books all the boasting, lies, taunting, curses and insults were taken up, they could scarcely be small books, rather they would be great volumes.

As for what pertains to the people, however, there are indeed many bad men

---

[275] That is, Luther's 1522 reply to Henry VIII after the latter wrote the *Assertio septem sacramentorum adversus Martinum Lutherum*, in 1521, 12 years before Henry himself would leave the Church. -Translator's note.

in the Catholic Church, but from the heretics none are good. And although this matter is well known to them, who knew the manners on each side, nevertheless they cannot bring themselves to condemn the testimony of Luther, twisted from truth itself. Afterwards, in a commentary on the Gospel for the first Sunday of Advent, he says: "The world becomes more degenerate, there are now men more desirous of vengeance, greedier, more removed from all mercy, more immodest and undisciplined, and more wicked than there were under the papacy." Thus Luther. This testimony is true, wherein there is little dissimilarity from the witness of Jacob Andrew Smideliwi, whose sermon on St. Luke[276] you may find partly in St. Peter Canisius' work, *De Corruptelis Verbi Dei*. Among other things, Smidelwi says about his own Lutherans: "So that the whole world will not recognize them to be Papists, they do not trust in good works, even inwardly they nearly exercise nothing of works. In place of fasting there are feasts, and they are idle in drinking feats of drinking night and day. Where it would behoove one to treat the poor kindly, they strip and flay them. They turn prayers into oaths, blasphemies, and curses of the divine name, and that so desperately, that Christ is not even so blasphemed by the Turks today. At length, in place of humility, pride rules everywhere, as well as wickedness, glorification, and all of this sort of life they say was instituted by the Gospel."[277]

I add even a third witness, that of Erasmus, who both knew their affairs well, and appeared to not altogether abhor their doctrine. In an epistle to Gerardus Geldenhouwer, which he wrote in 1529, he said: "Look around, this evangelical people, and observe whether they indulge less in luxury, lust and money than those do whom you condemn. Bring me the man that this gospel of yours should render from a reveler to a sober man, from cruelty to kindness, from rapaciousness to liberality, from curse to blessing, from unchastity to modesty. I will show you men who have become far worse." See also John Cochlaeus in his preface to the book of the deeds and writings of Martin Luther.

---

[276] *Sermon 4* on ch. 24 of Luke.

[277] Peter Canisius, *De Corruptelis Verbi Dei*, bk. 1, ch. 4.

CHAPTER XIV
The Eleventh Mark.

THE ELEVENTH Mark is the Glory of Miracles. There are two foundations which must be put forward. One, that miracles are necessary to new faith, or to persuade of an extraordinary mission. Two, that they are efficacious and sufficient, for we shall deduce from the first that there is no true Church with our adversaries, and from the second that it is with us.

Therefore, that miracles are necessary is proved in the first place from the testimony of Scripture. Moses was sent by God to the people, and said: "They will not believe me, and they will not hear my voice."[278] God did not respond that they ought to believe, whether they wish to or not, but he gave him the power of making miracles, and said: "That they might believe that the Lord had appeared to you." etc. And in the New Testament, "Going, preach, saying: 'The kingdom of heaven is at hand. Heal the sick, raise the dead, cleanse the lepers, cast out devils.'"[279] In John we read: "If I had not done works among them, which no other man could do, they would not have sin."[280]

Besides, one who is sent, ought to show testimony of the one who sent him, his authority, otherwise no one is compelled to receive him. However, everyone who is sent to preach, or is sent by God through ordinary prelates, or extraordinarily by God alone, and indeed, the one who is sent through an ordinary prelate, ought to show the testimony of the ordinary prelate, without a doubt, by letters fortified with his seal. One who is sent by God alone, ought to show the seal of God, which is nothing other than miracles. Thus it is said at the end of St. Mark: "These departed and preached everywhere with the Lord's help, confirming the sermon and following with signs." Also in Hebrews 2: "Contest God with signs and virtues."

As a sign that this is true, not only does St. Augustine say[281] that miracles

---

[278] Exodus IV.

[279] Matt. X: 7-8.

[280] John XV: 24.

[281] *De Civitate Dei*, bk 22, ch. 8.

were necessary that the world should believe, but even Philip Melanchthon concedes it, for he says that when there is a great darkness, new teachers are called, and miracles are always added by God, that we might know for certain that they were sent by God.[282]

Now what pertains to the second point, that a miracle should be a sufficient testimony, and where there is a miracle, there the true faith is, can be easily shown. Accordingly, true miracles cannot happen, unless by the power of God. Indeed a miracle is so called because it is above the strength of every creature, and therefore is miraculous to all creatures, and besides they are even called the testimonies of God in the Scriptures, as we saw above. Whereby, if something is confirmed by a miracle, it is confirmed by the testimony of God. God however, cannot be a witness to a lie, therefore what is confirmed by a miracle must be true. Moreover, it is not opposed that true miracles do not always happen to confirm faith, but merely to glorify the life of saints. For when miracles happen to show the glory of some saint, those miracles show that such a man was truly holy, although no man may be truly holy without true faith: "Because the just man lives by faith."[283] The same miracles show and confirm true faith.

With these foundations being placed, it will be easy to gather that the true faith is not found among the heathen, Turks, Jews and heretics, for they have no true miracles, and nevertheless, all these preach a new doctrine, and are not sent by ordinary prelates.

On the Pagans, it is known, for only trivial things are read, which can easily be done by a trick or by the demons, such as Valerius Maximus relates,[284] on statues and brutes speaking, or on a Vestal virgin drawing water with a sieve. Cicero reports of an augur who sliced a stone with a razor.[285] Tertulian in his Apologeticus, and St. Augustine in the City of God show how all these things were easily done by demons.[286]

On the Jews after the coming of Christ, it is known that they do not have

---

[282] Ch. 3 on Matthew.

[283] Hebrews X.

[284] Valerius Maximus, bk 8.

[285] *De Divinatione*, bk 1.

[286] Tertulian, *Apologeticus*, ch. 22 and 23; St. Augustine, *de Civitate Dei*, bk 10, ch. 16.

any miracles, and that one from the pool, which endured while Christ was preaching, afterward was lost.

On the Muslims, St. John Damascene says that Muhammad could prove his law by no testimony. The Qur'an itself confesses the miracles of Christ, but gives for itself a sword: nevertheless in ch. 64, it says once about the moon that it did some miracle, I do not know what since it was not expressed clearly. The expositors, however, say at some time the moon was divided into two parts, then Muhammad received it in his hands and renewed it, then returned it to the sky, but no one saw this miracle, except the author, that is, Muhammad.

Concerning false prophets and heretics, it is no less certain, that they often tried to do miracles, and were always frustrated in their hope. The history of the prophets of Baal is known, who wanted to call down fire from heaven through the invocation of Baal: nevertheless they could not, because the true prophet Elijah effected through the invocation of the true God in that business.[287]

Egesippus wrote that Simon Magus was deluded with equal reasoning, for he tried to rouse a dead man, and fly through the air, but succeeded in nothing.[288] The Manichees tried in vain to heal the sick son of a king, as Epiphanius writes.[289] Cyrol the patriarch of the Arians publicly blinded a certain man, who made himself to look blind and implored aid from him.[290] A certain Eunomianus was conquered by St. Macharius in a contest to raise a dead man.[291] The Monothelite, Polychronius, sweated in vain in the raising of another dead man, as the sixth ecumenical council attests in its public acts, no 15.

The Donatists performed miracles against themselves, as when they threw a vessel of chrism against a rock, which was held up by an angelic hand and could not be broken. On another occasion, they commanded the Eucharist be given to dogs, and they were torn to pieces by the same dogs.[292]

Theodore of Mopsuestia writes on Timothy Aeluro Eutychianus, that many nights he dashed about clothed in a black habit through the cells of the monks,

---

[287] 3 Kings, (1 Kings) XVIII.

[288] Egesippus, *de excidio Hierosol.* Ch. 2.

[289] *De haeresi,* 66.

[290] Gregory of Tours, *histor., Francorum,* bk. 2 ch. 3.

[291] John Cassian, *Collatione* 15, ch. 3.

[292] Optatus, *contra Parmenianum,* bk. 2.

saying that he was an angel sent from God, that he might signify for them, lest they might communicate with Proterius (who was the holy and Catholic bishop of Alexandria), and instead might designate him a bishop in place of Proterius.

Paul the Deacon writes on a certain Iconoclast that was enclosed in a certain tomb, then from there Constantine the Iconoclast began to convey praises upon him in heaven to which he responded, so that, without a doubt, it would be as though their heresies were confirmed.

The same thing is altogether certain on the heretics of our age. For, in the first place, Luther twice tried to perform a miracle: he wished at some time to cast the devil from one of his disciples, but he was in danger lest he be killed by the demon.[293]

Again (as John Cochlaeus writes in his acts of Luther for 1523), Nesenus miserably drowned in the Elba, with the hope of a miracle, Luther tried in vain to recall him to life with empty muttering. On the other hand, although Luther had not succeeded in miracles for the living, nevertheless after his death he showed a characteristic miracle. For when his dead body was carried in the middle of winter, in such a time when dead bodies are usually preserved for many days, he was closed in the best tin coffin so that he might be buried at Wittenberg. Yet, so foul an odor began to breath, that no one could carry him. Hence they were compelled to leave the body behind on the journey. See the little history on the death of Luther, which is usually joined to Cochlaeus' book on his life and acts.

Felicianus Ninguarda relates another miracle, in his book against Anne of Burgundy, and Lindanus in *Dubitantio*, as well as Alan Copus of a certain minister who, on the borders of Poland and Hungary in the year 1558 willed to raise a man by the name of Matthew, whom he had persuaded to contrive as though he were dead, and in reality he accomplished death.[294] The same story is told concerning Calvin by the same authors, but more completely by Jerome Bolsecus in his life of Calvin, ch. 13, from which we will place a few quotes.

"I ought not pass over his crafty and subtle plot, which he used at that time, when he intended to recall to life a certain man named Bruleus, from the country of Ostunum. For he undertook that he would obtain fame and a name for himself as a holy and glorious prophet of God, and an accomplisher of miracles. This is that history. That man, whom I said was named Bruleus from Ostunum, emigrated to Geneva, and since he and his wife were poor, they

---

[293] See Staphylus, who was present for a complete response.

[294] Alan Copus, bk. 6, *Dialogi.*

90

sought the favor of Calvin, that being commended to him, they might be made partakers of some savings for the poor. Calvin kindly promised them a subsidy for life if they would not deny a work which he wished to be performed in a certain matter through them. It would be beneficial for the faith, and required great secrecy. In turn they offered themselves to that which he requested of them.

Calvin had instructed that this wretched Bruleus should feign sickness. Then the ministers should commend them to the people in a sermon, that they might assist with prayers and almsgiving that they might succor their poverty. Not long afterward he put on the face of death and feigned that he was dead. Hence, Calvin being advised secretly, went out for a stroll as if he were ignorant of all these matters; furthermore, accompanied by a great throng of friends, at length he came to Bruleus' house, where he heard the shouts and wailing of the wife, who expressed how miserable and exceedingly desolate she was. He inquired what in the world might be the matter, entered, and suddenly fell on one knee, and the rest of the throng followed. Then Calvin implored with profuse prayers in a deep voice that God would show his power and restore this dead man to life, and that he would will to, so as to declare his glory to all the people, and together make himself (Calvin) manifest in particular, as his grateful servant, and to show that he was truly appointed to the reformation of the ministry of the gospel as well as of the Church. After such prayers, he approached the dead man, and while taking hold of the of the poor man with his hand, he commanded in the name of God that he would rise. Again he repeated, and more frequently the same words even with a deeper elevated voice. What happened? He [Bruleus] neither heard nor spoke, nor roused himself, for he was dead. By the Just judgment of God, therefore, who detests shams and lies, he who feigned death was found truly dead. The wife stirred him in every way, and struck him by every means, and she neither wrenched out a sound nor could effect that he move himself; rather he was all cold, wholly stiff. After this was recognized, she gave forth wailing in earnest and began from the depth of her spirit to attack Calvin, saying he was an imposter, a murderer, a thief, who killed her husband, calling from the order of the matter, in which she exposed the death with clear and loud voice . . . However much the servants of Calvin might wish to deny this, it was investigated and sufficiently recognized, and the truth of the matter was proved, nay more, confirmed through the wife herself."[295]

---

[295] Bolseco, *in vita Calvini*, ch. 13.

We can oppose to these what Tertulian says: "If they preach another God, why do they use things and letters of the same, against what they preach? If he is the same, how is he different? Otherwise, let them prove that they are new apostles: let them say Christ descended again, and gave to them the power of displaying the same signs. Therefore, why would I want to advance their virtues, except that which I recognize to be their chief virtue, which is a perverse imitation of the apostles? They raised men from the dead, these newcomers make dead men from the living."[296]

Calvin responds in the preface of the *Institutes* and in other places, that we injure him, because we are demanding miracles from them, while they merely preach the ancient doctrine, and innumerable miracles confirmed by the apostles and martyrs.

On the contrary: for we showed above that their doctrine is new, and opposed to antiquity. Thereupon it is certain that they at least teach something else than ordinary pastors of the Church teach. It is even certain that they are not sent by ordinary pastors, therefore we are not held to receive them, nor can we do so safely, unless they would prove their mission and apostolate with divine testimony.

Calvin responds: John the Baptist was also sent extraordinarily, and nevertheless he made no sign.[297]

But although John himself performed no miracles, nevertheless in that very matter, many and great ones were performed by God. First, that he was born from an old and sterile woman: thereafter, his father became mute, and after his tongue was freed in the birth of his son, which leapt in the womb, which from boyhood lived in desert places. From Luke's gospel, we learn that John was the son of a priest, and hence a priest and an ordinary minister. Besides, he taught nothing against the common doctrine, and did not separate himself from the rest of the priests and people. And although the princes and pharisees hated him, because he preached Christ, nevertheless, when interrogated by Christ, on what they thought about John the Baptist, they did not dare to reject him.[298] Thereafter, Josephus witnesses that John was held by the Jews to be among the

---

[296] *De praescript.*

[297] John X.

[298] Matthew XXI.

best of men, in view of his justice and righteousness.[299] Wherefore, the Centuriators lie when they say that John was held by the priests and the pharisees as a heretic.[300]

We come now to the second part, and we will show that our Church is the true Church of God from miracles, for there are many well documented ones in each age.

And first, from the eleven centuries, it is from the eleventh volume of the Ecclesiastical History of the Centuriators of Magdeburg; They record all of the miracles from the authors of those times, and in individual centuries they discover the many miracles in confirmation of our dogmas, such as sacramental confession, relics, images, the Eucharist, the Papacy, monasteries, invocation of the saints, etc., and they cite these titles.[301] And although they add on afterward that all of those were illusions of demons, or false stories, nevertheless they assert nothing, which is to say that they prove these miracles are opposed to the gospel of Luther.

It will be beneficial, nevertheless, to briefly record how the Church has been illuminated with miracles in all ages, so that even now we might understand that she is the true Church which is most like antiquity, that is, in which endures this gift. We have in the first century the miracles of Christ and the apostles, which are recorded in the Gospels and Acts.

In the second century we have the miracles of Christian soldiers in the army of Marcus Antoninus, about which you can read in Tertulian, Eusebius and other Fathers.[302]

In the third century, we have the miracles of Gregory Thaumaturgi, which are recorded by St. Basil, St. Gregory, Jerome and Eusebius.[303]

In the fourth century, we have the miracles of Anthony, Hilary, Martin, Nicolas, and others, written by St. Athanasius, Jerome, Sulpitius and others.

---

[299] Josephus, *Antiquities*, bk. 18, ch. 10.

[300] *Cent. 1*, bk 1, ch. 10, col. 363.

[301] Tomus XI, *Historicae Ecclesiasticae Magdeburgensium*, c. 13.

[302] Tertulian *ad Scapulum, Apologeticus*, ch. 5; Eusebius *Hist.*, bk 5 ch. 5; Oros, *hist.* Bk 7, ch. 15; the epistle of the emperor, which is joined to the works of Justin Martyr.

[303] St. Basil the Great, *de Spiritu sancto*, ch. 29; Gregory of Nyssa, *Vita*; Jerome, *de Viris Illustribus*; Eusebius, from the version of Ruffinus, bk. 7, ch. 25.

In the fifth century, we have many miracles, which Augustine writes down that happened in his time.[304]

In the sixth century, we have miracles, which St. Gregory relates in the dialogue, where he relates the deeds of two Roman Pontiffs, John and Agapetus.[305]

In the seventh century, miracles were done in England by St. Augustine and his companions, on which Gregory relates.[306] Likewise we read about King Oswald through the wood of the cross.[307]

In the eighth century, there are the miracles of St. Cuthbert and John in England, as Bede witnesses in his Ecclesiastical History.

In the ninth century, the miracles of Tharasius, written by Ignatius of Nicaea. Likewise there were other innumerable miracles of every kind done in the city of Soissons in the translation of the relics of St. Sebastian the martyr, which happened in the year 826. These were written in the annals of the Franks with supreme faith by the author, who flourished in that very time.

In the tenth century, the miracles of St. Romauld, written by St. Peter Damian. Also, of King Wenceslaus the king of Bohemia, and Udalrici and Dunstanus, the details of which can be read in Surius.

In the eleventh century, the miracles of king St. Edward who was a virgin, St. Anselm, Pope Gregory VII and others. Thus for the first eleven centuries.

In the twelfth century, St. Malachi and St. Bernard illumined the Catholic Church with miracles. St. Bernard wrote in the life of Malachi, bishop and papal legate, after he had related many of his miracles: "In what kind of the ancient miracles was Malachi not resplendent? If we will look at just a few things, which have been said, he lacked not prophecy, nor revelation, nor the grace of healing, nor the changing of minds, not even, at length, the raising of the dead."

Moreover, St. Bernard, a monk and father of monks, as well as being most devoted to the Roman Pontiffs, shined with many miracles, more than any of the saints whose written lives are extant. For in one day in the Diocese of Constance, it is certain that they gave sight to eleven blind men, cured ten

---

[304] Augustine, *de Civitate Dei*, bk. 22, ch. 8.

[305] Gregory, *Dialogus*, bk. 2, ch. 2 and 3.

[306] Bk. 9, epist., 58; Bede *hist.*, bk. 1, ch. 31.

[307] Bede, *Ibid.*, bk. 3 ch. 2.

crippled and eighteen lame, as Godfrey writes, who lived with him.[308] Besides all five of these books are so full of miracles, that it would be difficult to begin to count them.

In the thirteenth century, there were many famous Catholics in the Church, particularly St. Francis, whose life was full of miracles, as recorded by St. Bonaventure. Likewise, St. Dominic, whose life, although it was written more carelessly, nevertheless shows for certain that he raised three men from the dead. Others who were famous in the same century with miracles were St. Peter Martyr, and St. Thomas from the order of Preachers and St. Anthony and St. Bonaventure from the Friars minor, whose lives can be read in Antoninus' history.[309] At the end of the century, many famous miracles were done by St. Celestine V, both before and after he was Pope, as Cardinal Cameracensis writes in his life.

In the fourteenth century, there were also many famous for miracles, but especially St. Catharine of Siena, and St. Nicolas of Toledo, whose lives are also recorded by Antoninus in the aforementioned work.

In the fifteenth century, St. Bernadine of Siena and likewise St. Vincent, both living and dead were famous for many miracles, which can be seen from the same Antoninus, even that it is certain that men were raised from the dead through them.[310] The same St. Antoninus was famous for miracles in the same century, and his life is extant with Surius.[311]

In our own century St. Francis of Paul was famous for many miracles, as in the bull of canonization Pope Leo X wrote, which is extant in Surius. Our Blessed Father St. Francis Xavier, a priest from the Society of Jesus, was famous in India for every kind of miracle. It is certain from his Indian letters, which they, who lived with him, were sent to this place, and paralytics, deaf, mute, blind were all cured, the dead were recalled to life, and when he died he was conveyed to the island of Goa from Malacca, and he calmed the sea. Thereupon his body, after 15 months was untouched by death, and found to smell sweetly,

---

[308] Gotfridus, *vita Bernardi*, bk. 4, ch. 4.

[309] *Hist.*, 3 part, tit. 23 and 24.

[310] *Ibid.*, tit. 23, and 38.

[311] Surius (Lorenz Sauer), *de Probatis Sanctorum Historiis.*

although he was covered with lime for many months.[312] There is no doubt that even to this day [1590] he is preserved whole and incorrupt.

These are compared with the life and death of Luther. Luther left a monastery, married after a vow of continence, made war on the Pope; Francis entered a religious order, most diligently kept his vow of continence: obliged himself to the pope by a peculiar vow of obedience, and being sent by him, set out for the farthest shores of the world. Certainly these contrary journeys advance, that one or the other of them strayed from the right road. Who can be a better judge than God, who searches the depths and hearts of men? How could God openly express his opinion, by granting to one the singular gift of miracles and by preserving his body apart from the order of nature perpetually incorrupt, while at the same time another that could not raise a fly, and whose body began to rot immediately even apart from the order of nature, and at that in the middle of winter, when all things are stiff with ice, and so rotted that the stench could not be contained within the tin coffin?

Rightly, therefore, does St. Augustine say that he is maintained in the Church by the bonds of miracles.[313] Even Richard of St. Victor dares to say: "O Lord, if we believe something that is an error, we are deceived by you; for these have been confirmed among us by signs and miracles, which could not be done except by you."[314]

Yet, Calvin responds in the preface of the Institutes, and the Centuriators of Magdeburg in each of the Centuries, that the miracles of our saints are either made up or imaginary, or that they do not happen and are falsely told by historians, or if they indeed happened, they were tricks of the devil. Wherefore the Centuriators say, if those matters are true, which Sulpitius writes about the miracles of St. Martin, then no doubt Martin was a necromancer.[315] And indeed, they do not prove the miracles are false, they merely say so.

Moreover, they endeavor to prove they were the deceits of devils from the fact that, true miracles confirm the gospel, as is certain from the last chapter of Mark; these, so they say, overturn the gospel and confirm idolatry, that is, the cult of relics and images, the invocation of the saints, the Mass, and other things

---

[312] Lime hastens a body's decay. -Translator's note.

[313] *De Utilitate Credendi*, ch. 17; *Contra epistolam fundamenti*, ch. 4.

[314] *De Trinitate*, bk. 1, ch. 2.

[315] *Cent. 5*, c. 10, col. 1393.

of that kind. They add secondly, that from the miracles there is no supreme argument to prove truth faith, which they try to prove by four arguments.

First, because even Antichrist will perform signs and great wonders.[316]

Second, because Augustine says the Donatists were not to be believed even though they did miracles, where they called them in contempt "wonder workers."[317] Moreover, after he taught the miracles of the Donatists were not to be believed, he adds not even the miracles of the Catholics: "Such miracles, whatever they are, happen in the Catholic Church, therefore they must be approved, because they are done in the Catholic Church: The Church itself, however is not manifested, because these happen in it."[318]

Thirdly, that formerly at the tomb of Jeremiah miracles were performed, which were the works of demons. There it is clear, because they were done for the advantage of those who were worshiping Jeremiah for a God, with sacrifices and divine honors.

Fourth, because it is certain from Suetonius that the Emperor Vespasian gave sight to a blind man, and at one time healed a lame man. Likewise from Socrates,[319] the Centuriators advance the miracle of Paul the Novation Bishop,[320] although what they collected was not true religion, in which Vespasian or Novatian worshiped.

But we shall respond to each point. To the first, since they deny miracles to happen, which are related by our historians, I respond: They deny it shamelessly. It is foolish to believe Calvin and Illyricus more when they write on the ancient histories, when they were not there, than Bernard, Bonaventure or Anthony, who were there. Besides, as St. Augustine responded to the pagans who denied the histories of our miracles, "If it is allowed to deny former miraculous deeds without any reason, then not only shall our faith in all books perish and be abolished, but even of every other religion. Indeed, some gods are held, with works and wonders, written by learned men, they persuade the world

---

[316] Matt. XXIV; Apocalypsus XIII; 2 Thess. II.

[317] Tractatus in Joann, no 13.

[318] De Unitate Ecclesiae, ch. 16.

[319] Hist. Bk 7.

[320] Cent. 5, ch. 13, col. 1463.

of their divinity, whether true or false."[321]

To the second, when they say they are tricks of the demons, I respond: In the first place this is an old calumny, for in the same way the scribes and pharisees spoke about the miracles of Christ, and the pagans on the miracles of the martyrs, as they usually called them magicians and necromancers. Even the Arians, Eunomians and Vigilantians spoke thus about the miracles of Catholics, as Ambrose, Jerome and St. Victor attest.[322] Thereupon, it has no probability that St. Martin, Francis and certain others, who were very simple men, might have used magical arts.

But they say these miracles overturn the gospel. I respond: Indeed they do, the gospel of Calvin, that is not of Christ; furthermore they prove what these so boldly affirm. Nor is it less easy to prove the last argument, by which they prove miracles do not make certain faith.

To the first I respond. The miracles of Antichrist will be lies, as the Apostle says,[323] they are not true and solid, but appearances and wonders of men, nevertheless, not absolutely miracles, such as can be done through a craft of the demon. It is clear from the Apocolypse XIII, where for the greatest miracles of Antichrist it is proposed that he will make fire come down from heaven, and that an image of a beast might talk. This is easy for the devil, however, as is obvious. But the miracles of the saints are giving sight to the blind, curing the lame, raising the dead: which they cannot do except by the power of the one whom we sing of in Psalm CXXXV, "Who alone does great wonders."

To the second, I say: The miracles of the Donatists which Augustine condemned, were not such miracles such as are of the saints, but certain secret visions only, which they boasted that they had seen without any witness; such was the vision of Zwingli, who in the book titled, *A subsidy on the Eucharist*, he says he saw a spirit, but could not discern whether it was white or black; such was even the vision which is related in a book titled *Querela*, or *somnium Lutheri*, where Luther is related to have appeared to certain Lutherans, complained of them with sad countenance, because they were his disciples but were meaning to desert his doctrine in short order. Therefore, not without reason does St. Augustine call these sort of miracles fables.

---

[321] *De Civitate Dei*, bk. 10, ch. 18.

[322] Ambrose, *Serm. De ss. Gervasio et Prothasio*; Jerome, *cont. Vigilantium*; Victor, *de persequut. Wandalica*, bk. 2.

[323] 2 Thessalonians II.

On the other hand, Augustine makes the most of true miracles, as is clear from the City of God, where he brings in great miracles against the pagans, made by relics of the saints, especially of Stephen the first martyr.[324]

To that, which Augustine says, the Church is not shown from miracles but from the Scriptures, I respond. St. Augustine says the contrary in another place,[325] where he says "The Church can be shown from miracles, not from the Scriptures, rather, the Scriptures are shown from the Church." Lest, therefore, he might be opposed to himself, it must be said in each place he speaks hypothetically. Because, indeed, the Manichees admitted miracles, and denied the Scriptures (for they said the Old Testament was from the devil, and the new to be corrupted by falsifications), accordingly Augustine proved the Church from miracles, thus Augustine proceeds in another fashion against the Donatists, and from the Scriptures proves the Church, thereupon through the Church wishes miracles to be judged.

However, it must be observed that the Church is shown by miracles, and miracles from the Church, but in a different kind of proof; just as a cause is shown from its effect, and from the cause the effect. For from miracles the Church is proved, not with respect to evidence, or certitude of the thing, but in so far as to the evidence, or certitude of credibility. The reason of which is, because before the approval of the Church, it is not evident or certain concerning any miracle with the certitude of faith, it may be a true miracle; nevertheless it is such that evidently it should make an affair credible. And indeed, because it might not be evident, certainly because then the faith should be evident. That it might not be certain with the certitude of faith, is obvious, because it is not certain with certitude for us, to which it cannot be the basis of falsity, that it was not the illusion of a demon. Indeed, although the demon cannot make true miracles, nevertheless it can apparently do even the greatest.

Why, therefore (you ask) are they held to believe in the preaching of Christ, those who say his miracles? I respond: Because a man cannot be saved without the faith of Christ: and therefore he is held to receive that faith as a necessary means to his salvation. However, God refused to force men to believe unbelievable things, but only when through miracles, and similar motives was faith made credible: but from the Church the miracle is proved, in so far as it provides certitude of the thing, because when the Church declares a miracle happened, it is a true miracle, and we are certain that it is thus.

---

[324] *De Civitate Dei*, bk. 22, ch. 8.

[325] *Contra Epist. Fundamenti*, ch. 4 and 5.

To the third, I say: it is a lie of Calvin that the people worshiped Jeremiah with sacrifices and divine honors. For he brings no witness of this affair, except what he places in the margin (Jerome in the preface to Jeremiah). Besides, neither in the preface of Jerome for Jeremiah, translated by him, nor in the preface of the commentary of Jerome, is any mention made of this history. Besides that, it is recorded in certain other prefaces in the bibles of Benedict, prefixed to Jeremiah to what appears Calvin looked at. But this is not from Jerome, nor is any mention made therein of sacrifices or divine honors; but only that some miracles happened at his tomb. At length, Epiphanius and Isidore, in the life of Jeremiah, say that miracles happened, but they say nothing on sacrifices and divine honors.

I respond to the fourth: Neither a truly blind man, nor a lame one were cured by Vespasian. For as Tacitus writes, the doctors asked whether the plague was curable: they responded it was curable. He said: "The doctors disagreed in different ways, this man's power of sight was not wholly consumed, and if they could drive out the obstruction, if a healthy force might be applied upon the crook in the fallen limbs, he can be made whole."[326] Therefore it is no miracle, if the sickness is naturally curable, the works of the devil were cured. Add what Tertulian teaches in the *Apologeticus*, that it is believable that every plague was from the devil, who causing trouble in one man's eye, and another's shin, would impede the use of the members, and in the end, it would appear to be the healed when in fact they had ceased to harm them.[327]

To the last, I offer a response concerning the miracle of Novatian: the miracle was not in confirmation of Novatian's faith, but of Catholic baptism. Truly, Socrates writes on the miracle, that when a certain Jewish impostor came to the Novatian bishop, Paul, for the purpose of being baptized by him, so as to mock his own baptism, immediately all the water of the holy font vanished. But this was not a miracle of the error of Novation, but is clearly of the true baptism, wherein the same Socrates adds that it was recognized shortly after, that he was a Jew who had already been baptized in a catholic rite by Atticus, the bishop of Constantinople. Therefore, since God refused baptism to be so mocked, which is rightly maintained in the Church, he did not permit the Jewish impostor to be baptized again by the heretical bishop.

---

[326] Tacitus, *Hist.*, bk. 4.

[327] *Apologeticus*, ch. 22.

Chapter XV
The Twelfth Mark

HE TWELFTH Mark is the Light of Prophecy. Just as Christ promised in the last chapter of Mark the gift of miracles, so also does he promise the gift of prophecy, by means of Peter, in Acts II explaining the second chapter of Joel, which certainly is the greatest. Since it is certain, that no man can know the contingencies of things to come except for God: "Announce what is coming in the future, and we will know that you are gods."[328] And on the other hand, it was placed as a mark of false doctrine that a prophet would predict something, and it would not happen.[329]

Now among the heathen and the heretics, there were no true prophecies, but many false ones, unless by chance it came about in testimony of our faith, as were the prophecies of the Sybills and Balam. Albeit the heathen had many oracles of Apollo, nevertheless these were either ambiguous when Apollo in reality didn't know what might happen, or they preached what the demons were about to do; or those things which were beginning to come about they announced to the ignorant as things to come; or at length they preached those things which happen from natural causes unknown to us; that is by those things according to a greater subtlety of nature.[330]

The heretics also, as often as they wished to predict something were deceived. Clearly that is the case with the false prophets of the Old Testament.[331] In the New Testament period, at one time there was a man named Montanus, who wanted to be viewed as a prophet with two prophetesses Prisca and Maximilla, and they preached wars, and I do not know what other things to come; but the contrary happened, as Eusebius records.[332]

In our times, Luther, whom the Lutherans resolutely call the Apostle of

---

[328] Isaiah XLI.

[329] Deuteronomy XVIII.

[330] See St. Athanasius, *Vita S. Antonii*; St. Augustine, *de divinatione daemonum*; and Theodoret, *de Oraculis*.

[331] 3 Kings (1 Kings) XXII.

[332] Eusebius, *Hist.* Bk 5, ch. 16 and 18.

Germany, predicted it would come to pass that if he preached his doctrine for another two years, the Pope, Cardinals, Bishops, monks, nuns, towers, bell towers, the Mass, etc. would all vanish, and nevertheless he preached after that not two, but nearly twenty two years; he died in the year 1546, and nevertheless the Pope, Cardinals, Bishops, monks, etc. did not vanish.[333] Cochlaeus related on Thomas of Munster, who called himself Gideon, and armed numberless peasants against the princes of Germany: he predicted that certain victory was theirs, and moreover, in the morning they would remove all the throng of war-like tormentors. Instead, a little after they were slaughtered, and Thomas was taken and struck with an axe. Cochleaus relates further, that Lutheran prophets constantly asserted, that in a year the day of the last judgment was coming, and so marked the very day that they did not wish to seed or plow.[334] Nevertheless these were discovered to be lies.

But in the Catholic Church, besides the prophets of the old Testament, and those who were in the first five centuries from the coming of Christ, there were even true prophets and monks attached to the Roman Pontiff in later ages when, according to the Lutherans, the Church had perished. St. Gregory writes thus about St. Benedict: "Benedict reproved the king for his conduct, and he also foretold in a few words all the things which were going to happen: 'You do many wicked things, you have done many wicked things, now you rest for a time from iniquity. Indeed you will go to Rome, going across the sea, reigning for nine years, you will die in the tenth."[335]

On St. Bernard, it is written in his life, that he predicted to four men conversion, three thinking nothing of this, the fourth even less about the matter; all the things, as he had predicted, happened. But it is altogether wondrous, that the same thing is told about a certain nobleman; one of his sons asked St. Bernard that he would pray for his conversion, and the saint responded: "Fear not, I will bury him a real monk here in Clairvaux." How many prophecies are in this one statement? For both that he would at some time become a monk, and that he would persevere in the monastic order until death, and piously and uprightly was going to finish his last day before Bernard himself, and in Clairvaux, as well as that he would be buried by the hands of Bernard himself. There are six different prophecies among themselves, and nevertheless, all

---

[333] Cochleus, *in actis Lutheri anni 1525.*

[334] *Ibid.,* anni 1533.

[335] *Dialog.* Bk 2, ch. 15.

things were fulfilled with the singular providence of God. Thus indeed the author continues: "And he became a perfect monk, and was buried by his holy Father (as he had predicted) in Clairvaux: just as indeed he could not die with him away, he was sick for five months, and very quickly, rather immediately having the next response of death in himself, he held fast until his holy Father returned, who, as he once had promised, handed him over to burial.

St. Bonaventure writes on the life of St. Francis, that when the Christian army was going to join battle with the Saracens on a certain day, he warned the generals not to fight on that day, for it had been revealed to him by God, that the victory of the enemy was going to befall them on that day. But when the generals condemned the warnings of St. Francis, the Christians were cut down and scattered in an unheard of slaughter. Many other things of this sort can be added; indeed there are almost no holy men honored in the Church who were not glorified with this gift, together with miracles. But these few places will suffice.

CHAPTER XVI
The Thirteenth Mark

HE THIRTEENTH Mark is the Confession of our Adversaries. Truly, the force of truth is so great, that it even compels our adversaries to give testimony to it now and again, according to that which is read in Deuteronomy: "The Lord our God is not ours as their gods, and our enemies are judges."[336] Now, no Catholics have ever been found to have praised, or approved the doctrine, or the life of any of the heathen, or the heretics. Indeed we know there is only one true faith, and without it, there is no true justice. Therefore we firmly assert, that all err who do not follow our doctrine. The Pagans, however, or the Jews, Turks and heretics do not always speak thus about us.

From the Pagans there are many testimonies. Pliny the Younger wrote to the Emperor Trajan, that Christians detest every vice, and live in a most holy manner, and he could only reprove them in this alone, that they too easily poured out their life for their God, and because they rise in the hours before dawn to sing praises to Christ.[337] Tertulian witnesses, the Pagans refused to examine a case of Christians, but condemned them without discussion, for they knew that no evil would be found in them. Moreover, he affirms that those emperors who are reckoned to have been the best, favored Christians such as Marcus Aurelius, Vespasian, Antoninus Pius, etc., while those who were moved to persecute them are held to have been the worst emperors, even by the heathen themselves, as Nero and Domitian.[338]

There also exists a letter of the emperor Marcus Aurelius, wherein he witnesses when his army labored in Germany with great thirst for five days, and the Romans were surrounded by such a multitude of Germans, that it was impossible to escape by human strength. Then he had recourse to his ancestral gods, but in vain; thereafter some Christian soldiers, who were in the army, asked that they might pray to their God also. Next, they had scarcely gotten on their knee to pray when immediately a most joyful rain descended from heaven

---

[336] Deut. XXXII.

[337] Pliny the Younger, epist. Ad Trajanum, bk 10.

[338] Apologetics, ch. 1 and 2; ch. 5 and 6.

upon the Romans; but upon their enemies fire and hail were mixed. Tertulian calls this epistle to mind in the *Apologeticus*, and it has recently been discovered and printed in the works of Justin.

Thereupon, St. Anthony, St. Hilary and St. Martin were held in honor and reverence even by the Pagans, as Athanasius, Jerome and Sulpitius write in their lives.

We have from the Jews, in the first place testimony from Josephus, who affirms Christ was more than a man, and truly the Messiah.[339] Philo wrote a distinguished book on the praises of those Christians, who were living in Egypt under Mark the Evangelist. The aforementioned book was written on the praise of Christians, not on some Jewish sect, as the Centuriators reckon.[340] Many other writers reference this work.[341]

Muhammad in the Qur'an, chapter 2, teaches that Christians are saved, and in chapter 4 calls Christ the greatest of the prophets, and had the very soul of God. St. Bonaventure also records, that the Sultan of Egypt, although a Muslim, held St. Francis in the highest honor and reverence, although he knew that he was Christian and Catholic.

The same can be said concerning the heretics. For St. Gregory writes that St. Benedict, a Catholic, was held in such great honor by Totila, an Arian king, that he called him a true servant of God and a prophet.[342] Even Luther when he had already become a heretic, wrote thus against the Anabaptists, who rejected in hatred of the Pope the baptism of infants: "We affirm, that there are many good Christians under the papacy, nay more that every good Christian even from there comes down to us. By all means we affirm in the papacy there are the true holy Scripture, true baptism, the true sacrament of the altar, true keys for the remission of sins, the true office of preaching, true catechesis, as are the Lord's prayer, the Ten Commandments and articles of faith. I say, moreover,

---

[339] *Antiquities*, bk. 18, ch. 6. [Modern scholarship has seriously questioned whether this particular passage of Josephus is authentic, but no such doubt existed in the 16th century. -Translator's note.]

[340] *Cent. 1* bk 2, ch. 3, col. 18.

[341] Eusebius, *Histor.*, bk. 1, ch. 16; Epiphanius, *Haeres.*, 29; Jerome, *de viris illustribus* on Philo,; Sozomen, bk. 1 ch. 12; Bede in the preface on Mark.

[342] *Dialogue*, bk. 2, ch. 15.

there is true christianity under the papacy, the true center of christianity."[343] Where if he grants the center to us, certainly he preserves nothing for himself, except for the skin or the shell.

Calvin calls St. Bernard a pious writer.[344] But certainly Bernard was a papist, and no pious man is without true faith. Melanchthon, in his defense of the Augsburg confession, calls Bernard, Dominic and Francis saints, which Luther also did in his book on the need to abrogate the Mass, near the end. Likewise, as Cochlaeus writes in the acts of Luther for the year 1531, when, after many battles amongst Catholics and heretics in Switzerland, peace was settled, the heretics wrote that they wished to forgive their confederates for having remained in their true, unshakeable, and Catholic faith; but the Catholics wrote, that they wished to forgive their confederates for remaining in their faith, they added nothing about true unshakeable and catholic.[345]

---

[343] *Contra Anabaptistas.*

[344] *Institut.*, ch. 10 § 17.

[345] *Concordiae,*, art. 1.

CHAPTER XVII
The Fourteenth Mark

THE FOURTEENTH Mark is the Unhappy Exit, or End, of those who oppose the Church. Although God punishes them and scourges them, nevertheless at length he casts the chaff into the fire. "All ye nations praise His people, for he avenges the blood of his servants, and brings retribution upon their enemies."[346]

On the miserable end of Pharaoh, the first persecutor of the Church, we read in Exodus XIV. On Dathan and Abiron the first schismatics, we read about in Numbers XVI; on Jezebel, in 4 (2) Kings IX; on Antiochus, 2 Machabees IX; on Pilate, that he had killed himself as Eusebius writes.[347] He also relates the slaughter of the Jews which Josephus more broadly relates in his work *On the Jewish War.* Concerning Herod the Great, Josephus writes that he died gushing out worms since he had first killed his wife, and then his sons, and thereupon wished he had killed himself.[348] On Herod the Tetrarch, Josephus adds that he lost his kingdom and was relegated to perpetual exile where he lived most miserably.[349] On his daughter Herodias, see Nicephorus.[350] On Herod Agrippa see Acts XII. As for Nero, Domitian and the other emperors who persecuted Christians, all were cruelly killed, either by themselves or by others, or certainly perished miserably, as is certain from all the chronicles and histories. For Trajan was struck with a dreadful paralysis, and together with that died from dropsy. Diocletian gave up his empire on account of resentment, that he could not destroy Christians. Maximianus and Maximinus were struck with such dreadful sufferings that even the heathen doctors said it was a divine plague.[351]

---

[346] Deut. XXXII.

[347] Eusebius, *Hist.*, bk. 2, ch. 7.

[348] Josephus, *Antiquitat.*, bk. 17, ch. 9.

[349] *Ibid,*, bk. 18, ch. 14.

[350] Bk. 1 ch. 20.

[351] See Eusebius in his Chronicle, and bk. 9 *histor.*, last chapter.

Maxentius perished in a river and left behind a bloodless victory to Constantine.[352]

We come to the Heresiarchs and Apostates. Simon Magus, when he wished to fly, was knocked down by the prayers of St. Peter, broke his legs, and shortly after died with supreme ignominy.[353]

Manes was flayed alive by the king of Persia, not on account of faith, but because while trying to heal the son of the king he killed him.[354]

Montanus, Theodotus and their prophetesses killed themselves by their own snares.[355] The Donatists indeed threw the Eucharist to dogs, and were torn to pieces by the same dogs, as we quoted previously.

Arius wished to enter into a Church, but after a sudden movement of his stomach he went to the public toilets, and together with excrement all his intestines and his soul poured out.[356]

Julian the Apostate was killed by divine retribution, and lacked even a common burial; for the earth was opened of its own will, and he was swallowed, as St. Gregory Nazianzen writes in an oration that is found with Athanasius.

The Arian, Valens, who succeeded in the persecution of Julian, was burned alive by the Goths who were also Arians.[357]

Nestorius miserably died with his impious tongue consumed by worms.[358] Hunericus the king of the Vandals, an Arian and persecutor of the Church, was consumed with worms gushing through his whole body.[359]

The Emperor Anastasius, the patron of the Monophysite Heretics, was struck by lightning and died, as Cedrenus, Zonaras and Paul the Deacon write on his life. In the time of the Emperor Leo the Iconoclast, pestilence followed the

---

[352] Eusebius bk. 9, c. 9 from the version of Ruffinus.

[353] Egesippus, *de exicidio hierosolymitano*, bk. 3, ch. 2; Arnobius, bk. 2 *contra gentes*.

[354] Epiphanius, *haeres.*, 66.

[355] Eusebius, *Hist.*, bk 5, ch. 16.

[356] Athanasius, *orat.1 contra Arianos*; Ruffinus, *Hist.*, bk 10, ch. 13.

[357] Ruffinus, *histor.*, bk. 11, ch. 13.

[358] Evagrius, bk 1 hist. Ch. 7.

[359] Victor bk 3.

burning of images in the forum of Constantinople, which killed three hundred thousand people.[360]

Luther was taken up by a sudden death. For though he was happy and healthy and took up a splendid and rich supper in the evening, challenging all to a laugh with his jokes, nevertheless he died the same night. See Cochlaeus in the life of Luther.

Zwingli was cut down in war against Catholics, and a little after, his spiritual brother Oecolampadius of Basel, although he had gone to bed healthy in the evening, was discovered dead in his bed in the morning by his wife.[361] Andre Carolstadt was infected by a demon, as the ministers of Basel wrote in an epistle, which they published on the death of Carolstadt.

John Calvin was consumed by worms, and expired just as Antiochus, Herod, Maximinus and Hunericus, as Jerome Bolsecus witnesses in his life. Bolsecus[362] adds, that he died invoking demons, blaspheming and cursing.

---

[360] Mattheus Palmerius, *Chronica*, year 1241.

[361] Cochlaeus in actis Lutheri, anno 1531.

[362] It should be noted that Bolsecus (Bolsec), from whom St. Robert get's his information on these points, is prone to exaggeration. Bellarmine was a wise enough scholar to leave out the less savory accusations of Bolsecus and modern scholars question some of his accusations. Nevertheless, the biographers of Calvin record a painful death. -Translator

Chapter XVIII
The Fifteenth Mark

THE LAST Mark is the Temporal Happiness, divinely conferred upon those who defend the Church. Catholic princes have never so adhered to God from the heart as when they easily triumph over the enemy. In the first place, the victories in the Old Testament of Abraham, Moses, Joshua, Gideon, Samuel, David, Hezechiah, Josiah, and the Machabees are known. In the New Testament, Constantine, who was the first among the emperors to defend the Church, in that he conquered Maxentius in almost the same way as Moses did Pharaoh.[363] Augustine adds: "The Emperor Constantine was filled with so many earthly rewards, that no one is heard to desire the like, not by praying to demons, but worshiping the true God. One Augustus held and defended the whole Roman world. He was most victorious in administration and waging war. He succeeded above all in overthrowing tyrants. Old, he died from sickness and age, leaving behind sons as emperors."[364]

On Theodosius the Elder, St. Augustine also wrote that he was truly Catholic and pious, so much so that he fortuitously succeeded in everything, even in battle, the weapons of the enemies would fall back upon their authors, with God's aid.[365] Theodoret adds that the apostles, Sts. John and Philip, appeared on white horses in the same battle fighting for the emperor Theodosius.[366]

On Honorious, it is certain he was very attached to the Roman Pontiff, as is clear from his letters to Pope Boniface. St. Augustine writes that God so fought for him, that in one battle more than 100,000 Goths were laid low, and king Radagasius himself was captured with his sons and killed, while hardly a man was wounded or killed from the Romans.[367]

On Theodosius, the younger Socrates writes, that while his army was

---

[363] Eusebius, *Hist.,* bk. 9, ch. 9.

[364] Augustine, *De Civit. Dei*, bk. 5, ch. 25.

[365] *Ibid.*, ch. 26.

[366] Theodoret, bk. 5, *Hist.*, ch. 24.

[367] *De Civitate Dei*, bk. 5, ch. 23.

fighting with barbarians, meanwhile he was absent in the city in prayer with God, and around 100,000 Saracens were led by angels into the Euphrates, and perished miserably.

Justinian the Elder, while he was Catholic, most happily conquered, so that Italy, Africa and many other provinces were restored to the Roman Empire, as is clear from Evagrius.[368] But after he became a heretic, and wished to propose an edict that his heresy must be accepted, soon he was taken up by a sudden death, and freed the Church from a great fear, as the same Evagrius writes.[369]

Heraclius also, as can be recognized from John Zonara and other historians, while he was Catholic, carried back victory over the Persians, and recovered the cross of the Lord, when Roman affairs looked exceedingly desperate. But when he fell into the Monothelite heresy, all those things turned out unhappily, and he was cut down by an unheard of plague.

Likewise, it is certain from the histories of the Greeks, that the emperors of the east from that time, wherein on account of the tearing apart of images, separated themselves from the Roman Church, and day by day deteriorated more and more, until at length they nearly lost their empire. But in the west, it is manifestly gathered from the histories of the Latins, that their emperors flourished more and more, or less as they were more or less attached to the Roman Church.

In the time of Urban II, about the year of our Lord 1098, Christians, who were in a holy war decreed by the Pope for the recovery of Jerusalem, were in extreme desperation at Antioch, in that a numberless army of Turks and Persians were present, whilst they were too few, and daily exhausted by hunger, so that even very strong men leaned upon their staffs, and had but a few horses. It was so bad, that the general Godfrey, used a borrowed horse, and many princes were compelled to fight on donkeys. At length God revealed where the holy lance might be, and this being born before them, gave them victory in battle, so that they killed 100,000 Turks, and from their ranks hardly four thousand fell. Even a light rain divinely fell upon them, which added strength to their souls and bodies. At length three holy men appeared from heaven fighting for them.[370]

---

[368] *Histor.*, bk. 4, ch. 16.

[369] *Ibid.*, bk. 4, last chapter.

[370] See Paul Aemilius, bk. 4; William of Tyre, bk. 6, near the end; and Dodechinus, the continuator of Marianus Scotus.

In the time of Innocent III, 100,000 Albigensian Heretics were slaughtered in battle by 8,000 Catholics, as Aemilius Paulus records.[371]

In our own times, in the year 1531, five battles began for the Catholic faith in Switzerland with Swiss Heretics, and the Catholics always conquered, although they were inferior in number and arms.[372]

Charles V reported victory by a divine miracle over the Lutherans in the year 1547.

In France and the Netherlands Catholics brought back many victories over the Heretics, and not without a miracle. Nay more, the heretics were hardly ever superior when fought in battle. Moreover, these on the marks of the Church, and on all this disputation, have been said for the sake of brevity.

Laus Deo, Virginique Matri Mariae.

---

[371] Aemilius Paulus, *Historiae Francorum*, bk. 6.

[372] See John Cochlaeus in the acts of Luther, for the year 1531.

Made in the USA
Monee, IL
20 May 2020